THE NEW CHINATOWN

THE
NEW
CHINATOWN

Revised edition

PETER KWONG

HILL AND **WANG**
A division of Farrar, Straus and Giroux
New York

FOR DUŠANKA

Library of Congress Cataloging-in-Publication Data
Kwong, Peter.
    The new Chinatown / Peter Kwong. — Rev. ed.
        p. cm.
    Includes bibliographical references and index.
        1. Chinatown (New York, N.Y.)—Economic conditions.   2. New York
(N.Y.)—Economic conditions.   3. Chinese American—New York (N.Y.)—
Economic conditions.   I. Title.
    F128.64.C47K97   1996   330.9747'1—dc20   95-47731 CIP

Paperback ISBN: 0-8090-1585-4

ACKNOWLEDGMENTS
THIS BOOK is based in part on my experience as a long-time resident and activist
in New York's Chinatown. It is richer, however, as a result of my discussions with
hundreds of individuals, too numerous to record, many of whom are busy organizers
and community workers. They all supported my efforts to learn about their complex
community and were more than generous with their time and knowledge.
    I am especially privileged to have had the help of Wing Lam, a labor and community
leader in New York's Chinatown, and Glenn Omatsu, an experienced rank-and-file
union activist in Los Angeles. Through their work and experience they have arrived
at insights that related their day-to-day struggles to the larger political and social
developments in America. I owe them much for sharing their wisdom, and Glenn in
particular for his thoughtful editoral comments.
    I am also indebted to the Asian American Studies Center at UCLA for appointing
me a visiting professor, during the 1986–87 academic year, thus giving me time and
a congenial intellectual environment in which to complete my work.
    The New Chinatown is dedicated to my wife, Dušanka, who is the real writer in
the family. She has provided the editorial help and consistent moral support that
made this book possible.

                                                                                        P.K.

Designed by Mina Greenstein

12   11   10   9   8   7   6

CONTENTS

THE NEW CHINATOWN

INTRODUCTION

THE Chinese in this country have gained considerable prominence in recent years. Their image has undergone a drastic transformation. They are no longer viewed exclusively as workers in the restaurant and laundry trades. Today some commentators say they are "overrepresented" in Ivy League universities. Moreover, Chinese have earned distinction in elite professions, such as engineering and computer technology.

Chinese communities have mushroomed. Old Chinatowns in New York City and San Francisco have increased dramatically in population since the mid-1960s. New Chinatowns have been built in Miami, Houston, and San Diego, and suburban Chinese communities (Flushing in Queens, New York; Monterey Park in Los Angeles; Oakland in the San Francisco Bay area) have sprung up as satellites of long-established Chinatowns.

The success of so many Chinese and the growth of their communities have happened in a very short time. The increase in population alone is impressive. Beginning with the Immigration Act of

1965, the Chinese have come to this country in large numbers. Their population has increased by 241.4 percent—a jump from 236,084 in 1960 to 807,027 in 1980. In 1990, according to the census, the Chinese population reached 1,645,472, a 104.1 percent increase.[1] Today the Chinese are the second-largest immigrant group in this country after the Mexicans.

The increase in population has been extremely rapid since 1979. In 1965 the immigration quota for Chinese nationals was set at 20,000 per year; that quota included immigrants from both Taiwan and the People's Republic of China; there was an additional quota of 600 for immigrants from Hong Kong. Since the United States did not then recognize the government of the People's Republic, immigrants came mainly from Taiwan and from among Hong Kong residents who could claim mainland origin. In 1979 the United States and the People's Republic of China established formal relations and the country was given a separate annual quota of 20,000. The quota for Chinese has since been raised to 40,600 per year. However, since the children and parents of U.S. citizens and refugees are exempt from the quota, the total number of new immigrants may exceed that figure by 10 to 20 percent. And, of course, these numbers do not take into account immigrants of Chinese origin from Vietnam, Cambodia, and other parts of the world. At current rates of immigration, the Chinese population in this country will double every ten years. Few can keep up with the growth of Chinese immigrant communities; even fewer can foresee the impact of the Chinese on American society. Dealing with this question is as difficult as shooting at a moving target.

The influx has already brought misgivings. Some Americans believe that the Chinese should no longer be considered a disadvantaged minority eligible for affirmative-action programs. Others fear that immigrants are taking jobs away from Americans. Still others believe that the new immigrants are not interested in being assimilated into American society; they are often thought to prefer to live in ethnic enclaves, learning no English and putting up commercial signs in Chinese. The backlash has contributed to the passage of

English-only ordinances in many states, notably Proposition 63 in California in 1986, which stipulated English as the state's official language.

To many others it seems that the Chinese are doing so well precisely because they stick together. Most of all, the Chinese, unlike certain other minorities, are believed to be "making it" without depending on public assistance. They are willing to start at the bottom and help one another to get ahead. Thus, Chinese Americans are perceived as the "model minority."

This perception grossly simplifies reality. The Chinese today basically consist of two distinct groups. More that 30 percent are in the professional category (in contrast to less than 17 percent of the total U.S. population).[2] These Chinese, some of whom are American-born and others new immigrants, have more education and higher incomes that the national average. They do not live in concentrated Chinese ethnic communities. They are the "Uptown Chinese."

While the Chinese may be heavily represented in the professions, they are also overrepresented as manual and service workers; this group constitutes another 30 percent of the Chinese population. A significant proportion tend to be new immigrants, who are likely to live in Chinatowns, speak little English, and work at low wages in dead-end jobs. They are the "Downtown Chinese," who work as waiters and seamstresses.

The prevailing notion is that the Downtown Chinese willingly settle and work in Chinatowns, where they are protected by kinship and mutual-aid networks. Through hard work and cooperation, they create dynamic commercial and manufacturing centers in Chinese communities all across the country. The prosperity of these centers is thought to benefit all residents. Their successes have attracted entrepreneurs and investors from the Far East who, in turn, stimulate more growth and opportunities. The vitality of these communities can be measured by the increasing number of local banks and the remarkable jump in real-estate values, which in many instances are comparable to the highest in their respective cities. Some social scientists are so impressed that they consider Chinatowns "ethnic enclaves," a new route into the American middle class. It is a new route because immigrants can succeed without learning English and without joining the American labor market.

However successful Chinese communities may appear to outside observers, most residents are actually not succeeding. Hong Kong investors are attracted to Chinatowns because they provide ample cheap labor. Residents in the Chinese communities are still mainly working-class. A typical waiter employed by a Chinatown restaurant works sixty hours a week, for $200 a month, with no overtime pay, no health benefits, and no job security. Chinatown families live in run-down, roach-infested, three-room railroad flats, with usually three generations living together. They are not advancing economically; in fact, with the continued influx of immigrants, wages are falling and working conditions are worsening.

Economic hardship is to be expected for new immigrants who do not know English, lack marketable skills, and work in unstable industries. But many Chinese are also working for Chinese employers in an "underground economy": they are not protected by American labor law. Factory owners dodge social-security payments for their workers, landlords charge key money, Chinese-owned banks ignore banking regulations, youth gangs extort protection money from shop owners, and tongs intimidate—and even murder— dissenters.

Nobody dares to complain, because Chinatown is still dominated by a traditional political elite which, despite change, rules with the acquiescence of outside authorities. This structure was transplanted from feudal China during the late nineteenth century. Family, village associations, and secret societies were initially formed to defend immigrants against racial attacks from whites. However, these associations, once established, developed a strength of their own; they came to rule the working people in the communities. Today, this traditional order has been modified, but it continues to exist. It has adapted to modern conditions to serve a new class of owners and landlords in Chinatown.

By stressing the importance of the informal political structure and its firm grip on the destiny of many Chinese in this country, I do not wish to suggest that Chinatowns are so isolated that they are immune to outside influences. In fact, the militant civil-rights struggles of the 1960s had a major impact on Chinatowns, pressuring the federal government to set up Great Society-type programs. At the same time, a rising political consciousness among minorities has pushed for change. New political ideologies have penetrated deeply into Chinese communities. Civil-rights activists, social-welfare agencies, unions, and political parties are slowly eroding the power of the traditional order, but they have not yet displaced the hegemony of the Chinatown business and political elite.

The limited impact of forces for reform on the traditional order has to be seen in a larger national context. The American economy has entered a post-industrial stage, moving away from manufacturing into service and high-tech industries. Simultaneously, the American labor force is being reorganized, and the balance of power between business and labor has been altered. In this transitional period, employers are seeking cheap, immigrant labor. Thus, the American economic system has precipitated and encouraged exploitative working conditions. However, this exploitation is well disguised when Chinese work for a Chinese employer. Adding to this situation is the attitude of the American officials who generally do not intervene in the internal affairs of the ethnic communities. This benign neglect has only strengthened the dominance of the community's informal political structure.

To a certain extent, the situation facing Chinese immigrants is unique. Modern Chinatowns are not like black and Latino ghettos, which lack jobs and capital. Nor are they like the earlier European immigrant communities, which were essentially way stations leading to integration. The Chinese confront not only the racism of the larger society but also the dominance in their communities of a traditional political order.

Nevertheless, social change is taking place in Chinatown. Polarization has increased due to conflicts pitting Chinese working people against the Chinese elite. It is my intention to discuss the nature of this polarization and how changes are developing.

Overall, this book is optimistic, because I firmly believe, contrary to popular perceptions, that the Chinese are not docile. As new immigrants, the Chinese came to seek economic betterment, political stability, social justice, and equality. But, in fact, most end up having to work for others, own no property, and suffer exploitation and discrimination. Such circumstances require a certain show of docility or, at least, an ability to accommodate to situations created by others. Yet because most immigrants come to the United States under the most difficult circumstances, the average immigrant is likely to be both resourceful and assertive. The new immigrants, unlike their forebears, are not ashamed to receive social services and public assistance. While they may not be politically conscious in the conventional sense, they react strongly when confronted with injustice. Given able leadership, they are organizable. In 1978, 20,000 residents of New York's Chinatown demonstrated against police brutality.[3] In 1980, workers at the largest restaurant in Chinatown organized a successful strike which lasted over three months. Hundreds of supporters joined the picket lines. In the summer of 1982, 20,000 Chinese women garment workers demonstrated in support of their union contract when Chinatown factory owners refused to raise the minimum-wage level. This activism may lack persistence, but it is pervasive.

The working people of Chinatown are aware that they must rely on their own strength to solve their problems. They must build their own grass-roots organizations, independent of traditional forces. As their interests increasingly diverge from those of the elite, they must reach out to the larger society and form alliances with labor and political groups with similar class interests. Eventually they will be strong enough to challenge the dominance of the traditional Chinatown order.

I do not know whether Chinatowns will become integrated into the larger society, but I do challenge those who see this integration as inevitable, and I shall describe how many factors favor the maintenance of Chinese communities. Powerful interests in and out of Chinatowns are served by keeping the majority isolated from American society.

The exclusive focus of social scientists on the question of integration has had one important result. It has meant a lack of serious research on ethnic and racial communities, especially their internal dynamics. Conventional studies have tended to be superficial, describing communities from the outside by using statistics and census data. At best, they might interview certain important community leaders. This approach misses the nuances and dynamics of community life.

It is not enough to hear what leaders have to say; we need to explore the attitudes of different segments of the community. It is not enough to know that these segments exist; we need to understand their actions and interactions on complex issues. For this reason, detailed studies of ethnic communities are difficult and time-consuming. They are particularly difficult in the case of American Chinatowns, where the language barrier poses a major obstacle. Knowing Mandarin Chinese is not enough when most residents speak Cantonese and Toishan dialects. There is also the problem of studying a community divided into so many organizations and factions. Finally, few residents are willing to talk to outsiders. Most are reluctant to offer a negative image of the community for fear of retaliation or for reasons stemming from ethnic pride.

I lived in New York's Chinatown for many years, and worked for fifteen years as a community organizer in self-help programs, a food co-op, an English-language school, an independent restaurant union, and a grass-roots political party committee. I know the people and have close contact with residents. I also follow community developments through the nine local Chinese-language daily newspapers and by maintaining close touch with local reporters with whom I regularly exchange information.

This is not a book of success stories of Chinese Americans. It is about Chinese suffering under a dual form of oppression. My analysis is mainly based on New York's Chinatown. Since each Chinatown is different, it is difficult to generalize. However, almost all the modern-day Chinese communities have been affected by similar problems, such as rapid growth of population, economic expansion into manufacturing and consumer industries, the influx of overseas Chinese capital, the continued existence of traditional institutions, the emergence of class conflict, and the impact of social-welfare and labor organizations. By considering New York's Chinatown, we can gain insights into the nature of other Chinatowns as well.

THE OLD CHINATOWN GHETTOS

1

CHINESE who emigrate have the tendency to congregate in their adopted country. They seem to stay together much more than other immigrant groups. There are Chinatowns in every major city in Southeast Asia, and there are Chinese communities on the continents of Australia, Europe, South and North America. In the United States, there are dozens of Chinatowns, but they did not develop when the first settlers came here during the last century. The initial formation of Chinatowns in the United States was not voluntary.

FIRST SETTLERS: THE "COOLIES"

The California gold rush during the late 1840s brought the first wave of Chinese. When the rich surface gold mines were exhausted, most white miners moved on to more productive sites. Only

large mining companies had the necessary capital to work underground, and to realize a fair return, they needed a reliable supply of
cheap labor. "Coolies" ("bitter labor" in Chinese) from southern
China were brought to America as contract labor. By 1851 there
were 25,000 Chinese in California.

Once gold mining began to decline in the late 1850s, the demand
for cheap labor shifted to railroad construction. The second wave of
Chinese came to complete the most difficult section of the transcontinental railroad in the Sierra Nevada Mountains. They labored
under harsh and dangerous conditions, which few whites were willing to endure. Moreover, until the railroads were completed, workers
could not easily be supplied from the East. It was too costly to ship
black laborers to the West, around Cape Horn. Also, the use of black
labor was a sensitive issue due to the national debates on abolition
preceding the Civil War.

The Chinese—coming from a weak, stagnant, and partially colo-
nized Manchu empire—were substitutes for slave labor and were
treated accordingly. California courts at the time considered the
Chinese unassimilable aliens, without legal rights; they became the
targets of racially motivated ordinances and unfair taxation.

Once the railroads were completed, Chinese were needed to develop other Western industries. They built levees and reclaimed
marshlands for the delta farmlands of the Sacramento and San Joa-
quin river valleys, today considered among the most productive agricultural lands in the country; they were employed in salmon
canneries on the Columbia River, in Puget Sound, and in Alaska;
they worked in textile mills and in small-scale factories, rolling cigars,
sewing garments, producing silk, and making gunpowder.[1] By 1875,
Chinese laborers in the West had increased to 105,000 and constituted almost one-quarter of all able-bodied male workers in the state
of California.[2]

CHINESE EXCLUSION ACT

The Chinese at that point were becoming part of the American working class. This situation, however, changed when large numbers of white workers made their way westward on the newly completed transcontinental railroad. During the recession in the late 1870s, whites competed with Chinese for jobs. Employers hired Chinese at low wages, pitting them against white workers, and triggered a chain of reactions. The labor movement, then in its early stages of organization, considered the Chinese strikebreakers who cooperated with the monopoly capitalists. A group of skilled craft workers tried to use this anti-Chinese sentiment to gain political power. "Chinamen must go!" became their battle cry; racial demagoguery became the issue to rally white working people, many of whom were frustrated by unemployment. The Democratic Party, in the meantime, rebuilt itself in the West after the Civil War by shifting from its pro-slavery position to crude chauvinistic appeals. The period was marked by public hysteria over the specter of the "yellow peril." Finally, politicians from Western states, with the support of colleagues from the South, pushed the Chinese Exclusion Act through Congress in 1882. The Act barred all immigration of Chinese laborers. It was the first and, as it turned out, the only federal law ever to exclude a group of people by nationality.

The Chinese who were already in this country, including some 5,000 American-born Chinese, became the targets of abuse and mob violence. They were driven out of small towns and villages and sought refuge in larger cities. Thus, Chinatowns were formed in the 1880s— first in the major metropolitan areas on the West Coast and, later, in New York, Philadelphia, Boston, Chicago, Washington, and other cities.

The shift of Chinese into these urban ghettos was not voluntary. These were not like the immigrant ghettos of Italians, Jews, or Poles, which tended to disappear as each group integrated into American society. Rather, they were segregated areas where the Chinese were meant to stay. The segregation was maintained by the exclusion of

Chinese from the larger labor market. American capitalists had moved on to recruit cheap laborers from other Asian nations, such as Japan, Korea, and the Philippines.[3]

The Chinatown ghettos differed from the European immigrant ghettos in one other important aspect: the near-total absence of families. When the first Chinese coolies came to America, few women accompanied their husbands. After the 1882 Exclusion Act, the courts considered women laborers and they were excluded as well. The courts also refused entry to wives of those already here. As a result, the Chinese male-to-female ratio was 27 to 1 in 1890.[4] Because most states had miscegenation laws directed against the Chinese, the only way an immigrant could have a family was to go to China, marry, and return alone to the United States. Thus, Chinese males in this country, even those who were citizens, were likely to remain bachelors. Under such harsh conditions, some chose to go back to China to stay, and the number of Chinese declined to 89,863 by the turn of the century.

From 1900 to the 1940s, the Chinese population increased slightly, largely through illegal means. One common method of entry was the "slot system." Under U.S. law, all persons born in this country are automatically citizens, as are the children of citizens even if they are born abroad. Few Chinese at the turn of the century were born here. However, the San Francisco earthquake in 1906 destroyed most immigration and birth records. Thus it became impossible to disprove a Chinese claim to citizenship; a Chinese man could return to China and claim to have fathered a son, who could also claim citizenship. The "slot system" soon evolved into a lucrative racket in which individuals paid fees to become "paper sons" of Chinese Americans.

Not surprisingly, the harsh conditions of their working life and the intensity of discrimination caused many Chinese to view their residence in America as temporary. They planned to stay only as long as it took to save enough to retire in China as a small landowner. Few realized their dreams, yet this "sojourner" attitude discouraged them from wanting to be part of American society. They remained, living and working in Chinatowns.

ORIGINS OF EARLY IMMIGRANTS

Before the 1950s, most Chinese in this country came from the southern coastal province of Kwangtung (in Wade-Giles spelling; Guangdong in the Pinyin system used in China today), particularly from four small counties along the western region of the Pearl River delta near the city of Canton (the name given by Europeans; Kuangchou, the Chinese name since A.D. 210; Guangzhou in Pinyin). Land in the region was poor, and the population dense. The people were of peasant origin with little education; they spoke similar dialects and their cultural and social backgrounds contrasted sharply with those of the small number of Chinese who came to America as students.

During the period of exclusion (between 1882 and 1943), American law did provide temporary entry for certain Chinese, including merchants, government representatives, and students. By far the largest group was students, who came to earn advanced degrees. However, they were here under very strict provisions. According to the Immigration Law of 1924, students had to have completed a bachelor's degree in China and had to have their credentials accepted by an American institution of higher learning. They had to prove they were financially self-supporting and had sufficient funds to pay for their return to China within six months after graduation. They also had to have English-language skills. Not surprisingly, the majority were from wealthy and educated families. These well-to-do scholars and the Chinatown Chinese represented opposite poles of the class structure and had little to do with one another. Furthermore, most of the students were non-Cantonese-speaking. Even those who were Cantonese tended to be graduates of elite colleges located in commercial and cultural centers like Shanghai, Peking, Tientsin, Nanking—mostly cities north of the Yangtze River.

Very few students wanted to stay in the United States after graduation. For one thing, they faced an inhospitable racial environment; they could not get jobs, despite their graduate degrees. On the other hand, good positions awaited them in China. According to a study

by Y. C. Wang, based on *Who's Who in China,* by 1939 56.2 percent
of the highest-ranking figures in the Chinese Nationalist government,
academic institutions, and the military had received advanced education in the United States.[5]

In contrast to the students, the vast majority of the residents of
old Chinatowns came from a homogeneous agrarian background.
Their common rural origin had important implications. First, it enabled immigrants to form tightly knit communities capable of de-
fending themselves against hostile external forces. Second, the formation of political and social institutions in Chinatown was based
on the regional and agrarian traditions of Kwangtung. The result is
an internal structure in Chinatown that is difficult to penetrate, even
for Chinese of non-Cantonese origins. Once these institutions, with
their distinctive regional traits, became consolidated, they were maintained even after the population of Chinatown became diversified.
Therefore, in order to understand Chinese communities in this country, it is essential to appreciate the unique qualities of the Cantonese,
the original Chinese immigrants of the last century.

THE UNIQUE
CANTONESE

To Chinese from other provinces, Cantonese are unique. They
speak a dialect which is one of the most difficult for those in other
areas to understand. Kwangtung Province was first incorporated into
the Han cultural and political system in the seventh century A.D.
during the T'ang dynasty.[6] The original inhabitants were tribal ab-
origines of the Miao, Li, Yao, and Thai people. The city of Canton
for centuries was considered by the Chinese to be a backwater; for
a millennium it was the place of exile for officials who had lost
imperial favor. Canton was isolated from the rest of China. Land
travel to the area was obstructed by a ring of high mountains. A
railroad connecting Canton and central China was not completed

until 1936. Before then, the sea was the main link with the rest of the country.

As early as the seventh century Canton was an important international port for Arabic, Jewish, Singhalese, Indonesian, and Persian traders who came to buy Chinese slaves as well as silk, porcelain, and other goods. In the sixteenth century, European traders began to arrive. Later the Ch'ing government (1644–1911) restricted all foreign trade to the port of Canton, in order to keep foreigners as far as possible from Peking.

The Cantonese, therefore, experienced an early and extensive Western penetration. A systematic foreign trade developed. Chinese merchants, called *cohong*, monopolized the trade and made millions. The British and Americans shipped opium into China. This lucrative scheme eventually precipitated the Opium War (1839–42). The immediate cause was the confiscation of a shipment of British opium imported into Canton by Lin Tse-hsu, the Viceroy of Kwangtung and Kwangsi Provinces. The Chinese held their ground when the first battles were fought in Canton, but lost the war when British warships turned north to invade the city of Nanking. China's defeat in 1842 forced her acceptance of Western supremacy. China agreed to open five trading ports, Canton included, and to relinquish territories. Hong Kong, an island at the mouth of the Pearl River near the city of Canton, became a British colony.

Military defeat was followed by drastic economic decline. Famine and starvation led to a series of peasant uprisings in the south. Local warfare spread across the region. One group that suffered greatly during this period was the Hakka (the "guest people"), who had come to Kwangtung from the northern plains to escape economic hardship in the fourth century. They had settled in the poor, mountainous areas of the province. When they periodically tried to move to more fertile regions, they faced serious conflicts with the Punti (the "local people").

The Hakka were the main organizers of the Taiping Rebellion (1848–65), which almost succeeded in overthrowing the Ch'ing Dynasty. At one time, the rebels occupied the southern half of the country. The revolt began in Kwangtung, but fighting spread throughout China. In the meantime, warfare flared up again between the Hakka and Punti. For thirteen years (1854–67), while the Ch'ing government was busy dealing with the Taiping rebels, the two peoples waged a devastating struggle for control of the southwestern corner of the Pearl River delta. An estimated 500,000 people were killed. The Punti formed their own militias, built walled fortifications, and hired mercenaries. The people of both sides suffered grievously.

Thus, the Cantonese experienced civil wars, plundering by local bandits, and foreign invasions—all without the protection of the central government. They had to rely on their own resources to defend themselves and to survive. It was during these years that the Cantonese from the warring region migrated in large numbers to foreign lands. Many from Toishan, where the Punti-Hakka warfare was most intense, came to the United States.[7] Previously, the Ch'ing Dynasty had prohibited its citizens from leaving the country, to prevent them from joining the forces still loyal to the previous Ming Dynasty which had bases on offshore islands. However, when the Opium War opened the gates of the empire, the government was too weak to control the exodus.

In the nineteenth century the Cantonese and the Fukienese (from the adjacent coastal province to the north) were practically the only groups that chose to emigrate. They were peasants who left China with the expectation of making enough money to help support their families. Once overseas, a few, especially those who went to Southeast Asia, became prosperous merchants and small businessmen.

Cantonese are known as good businessmen—a reputation acquired from their commercial heritage. They are said to be worldly, shrewd, quick to learn, and willing to accept new ideas.[8] However, shrewdness in business was not respected in traditional Chinese society. According to the Confucian social structure, merchants were in the lowest rank. Chinese from other provinces regard the Cantonese as too direct, at times hot-tempered, always ready to defend their own interests, and lacking in proper Chinese culture and civility.

The Cantonese in turn claim that their dialect, uncontaminated by foreign influences, is closest to archaic Chinese. (Many words used by the Cantonese no long appear in modern Chinese dictionaries.) They also maintain that family ties, the basis of Chinese culture, are stronger in Kwangtung than anywhere else.[9]

As for civility, the Cantonese think the northerners are stuffy and pretentious. My Cantonese waiter friends often complain about working with northerners, particularly from Peking or Shanghai, who feel compelled to explain that they are above restaurant work and that they are doing it only temporarily. The Cantonese call them *ng soung*: uptight. The Cantonese are not ashamed of performing manual labor or engaging in trade. They are not as status-conscious as northerners and are willing to accept paths to upward mobility other than the traditional Confucian scholar one.

In any event, the Cantonese are unique and are treated by other Chinese as such. As a result, historically they have turned inward and relied on their most basic resources: their families, local clans, and village associations. People from Kwangtung have the strongest clan and lineage ties of all Chinese. They maintained them when they moved to urban centers in northern China, and also when they emigrated to foreign countries. Above all, the Cantonese tend to stick together. Thus, they are considered clannish. But this behavior has little to do with respect for tradition; it is a practical strategy for survival in a hostile environment.

The Cantonese in America could not count on help from their home government regarding their discriminatory treatment in the United States, because China as a nation was too weak throughout the late Ch'ing and the subsequent Warlord and Civil War periods from 1911 to 1949. The isolation of the early immigrants in America was complete; they were excluded by American society, persecuted by American authorities, ignored by the Chinese government, and seen as "marginal" people by their fellow Chinese. These were the perceptions of the early immigrants as they built the social and political institutions within their Chinatowns.

WORLD WAR II AND
THE CHINESE
COMMUNITIES

World War II brought changes in the status of the Chinese in the United States. When China became an ally of the U.S., there was a surge of respect from Americans for the long struggle of the Chinese people against Japanese aggression in Asia. This new attitude was reflected in 1943, when the Chinese Exclusion Act was repealed. After more than sixty years, Chinese were allowed to enter the United States, although under a yearly quota of a mere 105 persons. During the wartime labor shortage, the U.S. government prohibited racial discrimination in defense-related industries. Chinese worked in factories and gained experience in skilled trades; many kept these jobs after the war as discrimination in employment gradually lessened.

The government also promoted family unity by taking steps to change the law, so that Chinese with American citizenship could bring their wives to this country. Further, the War Brides Act allowed those in the Armed Forces to bring spouses into the United States. By 1947, approximately 9,000 women had come; 80 percent of all Chinese immigrants who entered between 1945 and 1947 were women. These measures eased the extremely imbalanced sex ratio in the Chinese community. By 1950 the ratio had improved to 1.89 males to 1 female. However, for those between the ages of thirty-five and thirty-nine the ratio was 3 to 1; and for those aged sixty-five and above, the ratio was 6 to 1.[10]

Those who were able to bring their families to America no longer considered themselves sojourners. They determined to settle down, raise children, and become part of American society. However, the most decisive change in American immigration law came in the 1960s.

THE IMMIGRATION
ACT OF 1965

In 1965 a new immigration act ended the discriminatory national origins provision established in 1924. That provision had assigned to each country an annual quota based on the national origins of the population in 1890 (Chinese theoretically had a quota, but it was withheld until the repeal of the Exclusion Law in 1943). The provision had been enacted in 1924 in order to preserve the racial and ethnic character of the country. As a result, 94 percent of immigration quotas were assigned to the countries of Northern and Western Europe. The 1965 Act abolished that stipulation, substituting a flat quota of 20,000 immigrants for every country outside the Western Hemisphere, without regard to race and nationality.

The passage of the 1965 Immigration Act was the result of the changing race relations in America that began in the 1950s. The black struggle for equality heightened awareness of other "colored" minorities—Chicanos, Puerto Ricans, Native Americans, and Asians. Beginning in the 1960s, government social-welfare programs began to list these minorities, along with the blacks, as "disadvantaged," deserving of assistance to correct discrimination.

At the very time that blacks were demanding civil rights, ethnic whites of Southern and Eastern European origin were fighting for their own rights in employment, housing, and other matters. One of their main concerns was the abolishment of the 1924 Immigration Act, which contained the national origins provision. Poles, Italians, Greeks, Jews, and others rallied around the new 1965 Immigration Act.

The ethnic whites did not take full advantage of the new law, because by the mid-1960s Europe's economy had generally improved and few felt the need to emigrate. The greatest beneficiaries were Asians and Latin Americans. But the spirit of equality reflected American attitudes toward colored immigrants, who had been systematically restricted from entering the country. The new immigration act represented a liberal and enlightened vision, and it was no accident that it was passed in 1965, one year after the Civil Rights Act of 1964. Both were intended to make America a color-blind society.

The new law profoundly affected the composition and the size of Chinese communities. The Chinese population increased dramatically: from 236,084 in 1960 to 1,079,400 in 1985. Today, the Chinese are the largest Asian group in the United States.

According to the 1965 act, preference for admission emphasizes two principles: first, to unite the families of American citizens; second, to admit persons with professional skills needed in the U.S. economy. These categories foster two very different types of Chinese immigrants. Those who arrive with professional skills are better able to integrate into the American society and do not settle in Chinatowns. They are the Uptown Chinese.

While the 1965 Immigration Act favors professionals, 74 percent of the quota is actually reserved for the relatives of American citizens. Since most citizens of Chinese descent were traditionally of humble origin, mainly from the rural areas of southern China, their relatives are likely to have similar backgrounds. Immigrants in this category tend to settle in Chinatowns with their sponsoring relatives. They comprise the Downtown Chinese.

Despite the rising status of the Chinese in American society, large numbers of new immigrants have chosen to remain in Chinese communities. Chinatowns across the country have experienced rapid expansion. Old Chinatowns in cities like New York, Los Angeles, and San Francisco are bursting at the seams. New communities are springing up everywhere.

The gravitation of new immigrants toward Chinese communities, despite the breakdown of racial barriers in the larger society, can still be attributed to their need for mutual support. Concentrated immigrant communities are not new in America; they provide a familiar environment for newcomers without jobs and English-language skills. But the basic assumption is that they provide only *temporary* quarters.

Most Americans who believe that today's Chinese immigrants should follow the path of the early European immigrants ignore the similarities of Chinatown to black and Latino ghettos. It is widely believed that immigrants should assimilate and make every effort to become "American." They should first learn the language, even if it means going to night school after a long day of work. They should appreciate hot dogs and understand baseball. Above all, they should avoid hanging around their countrymen too much. Ethnic ghettos may exist, but they should be a transitional stage, serving as a home for newcomers until they learn English and adjust to the American culture.

The argument seems logical, because immigrants customarily have found work outside their ethnic communities. In the long run, the location of the workplace determines where people live. Once better jobs are found, the newcomers move on and the ghettos slowly wither away. Most immigrants want to get out of their ghettos as soon as possible.

Most of today's Chinese immigrants not only live in their ethnic communities, they also work there, and maintain a high degree of isolation from the rest of American society. Some observers suggest that this reflects the Chinese desire to maintain their culture and tradition—an admirable trait to those lamenting the disappearance of ethnic diversity. Others consider the separation as un-American— a refusal to become part of this country.

In the past Chinese were, as we have seen, sojourners, for the most part unwilling to be a part of American society. But this is not the case with recent immigrants who arrive with permanent resident status. They are overwhelmingly young couples with children; they have no intention of returning to China; they want to stay here.

What is distinctive about America's Chinatowns today—in contrast to the black, Latino, and even earlier European immigrant ghettos—is the dynamic growth of industries and commerce. Immigrants are attracted by jobs. Once they settle in these communities, the Chinatowns' economic and social system holds them in. Normally we think of an immigrant as an individual confronting the whole American society. His eventual assimilation is a foregone conclusion. However, the development of Chinatowns today is different.

New York's Chinatown is the largest Chinese community in the country, and it is still growing. Its population in 1940 was 11,000. The unofficial count for 1985 was 100,000: 70,000 residents and 30,000 non-residents working in the community. According to the Chinatown Planning Council, there are approximately 1,400 new arrivals each month from Taiwan, Hong Kong, and the People's Republic.[11] While many aspects of New York's Chinatown are understandably unique, the major characteristics of its present growth are shared by the other Chinatowns.

ECONOMIC BOOM IN NEW YORK'S CHINATOWN

2

Before the mid-1960s, New York's Chinatown had a small, "pre-capitalistic," service-oriented economy. At its peak, the community encompassed only a six-block area, with a population never exceeding 15,000. Today its population has grown more than sevenfold, and is still increasing. According to a survey by the U.S. Immigration and Naturalization Service, New York is the first choice of Chinese immigrants. From 1965 to 1977, 22 percent of all Chinese, before their arrival in America, selected New York City as their destination.

The attractiveness of New York is understandable, since it is the largest metropolitan center in America. Immigrants come expecting a greater availability of jobs. Most of the Chinese immigrants, however, look for jobs almost exclusively in Chinatown. They have learned through the grapevine that it is easier to find jobs there than anywhere else. The 1980 U.S. Census seems to validate this claim. It showed that New York's Chinatown has an extremely low unemployment rate:[1] 3.4 percent compared to the national average of 6.4 percent, and even lower than Chinatowns in Los Angeles (4.5 percent) and San Francisco (5.2 percent).* Above all, the businesses of New York's Chinatown have shown an ability to create jobs for new immigrants. According to the same census, 80.4 percent of the population of Chinatown were foreign-born, and 21.9 percent had lived there for fewer than five years. In addition, 54.8 percent did not speak English well, or at all, and 71.4 percent had not finished high school.

The most distinctive feature of New York Chinatown's economy is that people find jobs within the community, working for Chinese employers. Two major industries provide the majority of jobs: some 450 restaurants employ approximately 15,000 people, mostly men; some 500 garment factories employ around 20,000 Chinese women. A new immigrant can usually find work through want ads in Chinese-language newspapers, through Chinese employment agencies, or from help-wanted notices posted on garment-factory doors or in restaurant windows.

These two industries provide the basis for the development of related businesses. A vertically integrated network of suppliers has evolved to serve Chinese restaurants: Chinese wholesalers provide vegetables; they, in turn, get their supplies from Chinese-owned farms in New Jersey and Florida; bean curd and soy-related products come from local soybean factories; canned mushrooms, bamboo shoots, and other foods are imported from China by import and export firms; noodles and dumpling wrappings are made in Chinese noodle factories; signs and interior construction are carried out by Chinese companies with Hong Kong–trained carpenters; menus in English and Chinese are printed by Chinese print shops (the reason why one finds so many amusing misspellings in English and strange names of dishes). Commercial tableware, industrial stoves, and kitchen equipment formerly had to be purchased from American wholesale

* These statistics have to be qualified by another question asked about employment conditions in 1979. A 1979 study showed that a much higher percentage of Chinese in Chinatowns in contrast to white Americans experienced at least one week of unemployment in 1979. This seems to indicate that while the Chinese were generally employed, they changed jobs often, reflecting the unstable nature of Chinatown job markets, but also their need to remain in that job market.

firms. Today, Chinese merchants have taken over half of these firms on the Bowery. This extensive local network makes starting a restaurant much easier and encourages business investment. A similar network exists in the garment industry, where there are several Chinese-owned industrial sewing-machine and parts dealerships and wholesale textile and fabric companies.

Chinatown, therefore, is able to develop new business opportunities from its established enterprises. Economists call this phenomenon the "multiplier effect." The capacity to expand economically and to create new jobs is unusual for an immigrant community, which normally suffers from a shortage of capital.

There are various explanations why this expansion is taking place in Chinatown. Some suggest that the answer is cheap labor. Most Chinese immigrants know little English and have few marketable skills. Like most immigrants, they must work hard, usually for very low wages. However, cheap labor also exists in other immigrant and ghetto areas; it does not necessarily create jobs, unless it can serve a growing economy.

Another fashionable theory is that the Chinese are prosperous because they are willing to work with one another by pooling their resources through mutual-aid, clan, and village associations. The problem with this theory is that mutual aid has long existed in Chinese communities; it does not explain why an expansion of the Chinatown economy did not occur earlier. When Chinatown's economy was at a pre-capitalistic stage of development, business success brought benefits to a limited number of individuals at best; it never provided impetus to the kind of transformation going on today.

Restaurants, laundries, groceries, and gift shops were the main businesses in the Chinatown of the past. These were all small-scale operations. Groceries and restaurants had an average of six employees, rarely more than twelve; almost 75 percent of the laundries were one-man or, rather, one-family operations.[2] The only large businesses were noodle factories, food wholesalers, and machine wet-wash factories (industrial-size laundries).[3] Even they were larger only in revenue, not necessarily in the number of people employed.

Business practices then were conservative. In the early 1960s the Chinese-language *Mei Chou Daily* carried an editorial which lamented that everybody in Chinatown engaged in small-service and retail trades, resulting in "hundreds of restaurant and laundry establishments, thus suffering from cutthroat competition. And yet few look to capital-intensive enterprises as an alternative." The reason, the editorial continued, was that the Chinese had yet to develop the know-how and the ability to raise necessary capital in order to adopt mechanization and scientific management.[4] Without these resources, even a well-run business would be limited and could create very few jobs.

Today, the Chinatown economy is able to absorb thousands of immigrants. Its large-scale enterprises have established a foundation for the development of a multitude of consumer-service and white-collar jobs. Clearly, somewhere along the line Chinatown has found the resources to make the transition into a modern capitalist economy.

A recent popular notion explaining the growth in Chinatown cites the influx of funds from the Far East but overlooks the fact that Asian investment came only when there was promise of sufficient return on capital. The "takeoff" period of Chinatown's economic expansion occurred *before* the massive flow of foreign capital.

The transformation of New York's Chinatown came as a result of a complex of reasons. No single factor was the prime cause; expansion occurred in a step-by-step process.

The growth began in the early 1960s. By that time, the traditional industries in Chinatown were in serious trouble. The hand-laundry industry, which provided a livelihood for many Chinese, was in a decline because of the introduction of modern press machinery by American competitors. Also, many middle-class families purchased washers and dryers for their homes. Without sufficient business, hundreds of small laundries were put up for sale. Those that remained faced hard times. Some older laundrymen recall that in the sixties they had to work sixteen hours a day, seven days a week. To most, the memory of getting up each morning to iron more than one thousand shirt collars by hand in one day is still a nightmare.

In the meantime, restaurants, the other main source of jobs for the Chinese, were not doing much better. They could not expand because of Chinatown's dilapidated physical condition. In fact, more than once, the Housing Division of New York State presented a "Chinese Village Plan" to the City Board of Estimate—a plan to beautify Chinatown in order to attract more tourists.[5]

It was during this difficult period that the garment industry moved to Chinese neighborhoods, where it was fundamental in transforming the economy.

CHINESE WOMEN WORKERS HOLD UP MORE THAN HALF THE SKY

Since World War II Chinatown has experienced a dramatic social change brought about by the large influx of women, a result of the War Brides Act in the late 1940s and the "Uniting the Family" provision of the 1965 Immigration Act. In a very short time Chinatown was transformed from a bachelor society to a family-oriented community.

In the short run, the sudden influx of women and children into Chinatown further depressed the community's standard of living. A number of social-welfare studies have shown that Chinatown in the 1960s had a high percentage of residents living below the poverty level, in substandard, overcrowded housing, and with inadequate health care, education, and social services.[6]

It was soon evident that the newly arrived women were eager to work. Some 75 percent were between the ages of sixteen and sixty-four. Many had young children, but on the whole they provided a large pool of labor, ready to work in order to supplement family income. As it happened, opportunities opened up in the garment industry.

New York has historically been the center of the American garment business. It has had the advantage of having a seemingly endless source of immigrant women laborers. In the 1960s, however, the

New York garment industry declined because of competition from
Southern states and Third World countries. Between 1969 and 1982,
the number of jobs in the midtown garment center fell by almost
40 percent. Today this decline has been reversed. New York has
regained its leading position in the nation. Ironically, a study commissioned by the International Ladies Garment Workers Union and
the New York Skirt and Sportswear Association showed that "central
to the revival of the industry's fortunes in New York City has been
the emergence and growth of the garment industry in Chinatown."[7]
During this period, the number of Chinese women working in New
York's Chinatown garment factories increased from 8,000 to 20,000.

In the 1960s, the New York midtown garment industry lost large
numbers of skilled and experienced Italian and Eastern European
women because of retirement. The recruitment of workers from
minority communities was unsuccessful, because the migration of
Puerto Ricans and blacks from the South slowed down. Sporadic
layoffs and lower wages, conditions common to the industry, de-
terred new workers from entering it. In addition, the rising level of
public and welfare assistance in the 1960s made working in low-
wage sweatshops unattractive. Further, there was little incentive for
those in the industry to be committed to their jobs.[8] Actually, the
New York garment industry suffered from a shortage of labor.

Chinese women of working age with families were in a different
position. As recent immigrants, they did not speak English but sought
employment to provide extra income for their families. They were
willing to work for low wages and to tolerate seasonal layoffs. Furthermore, the International Ladies Garment Workers Union, which
recruited Chinatown garment workers, offered full health insurance
for their families. This factor alone tied many women to the industry,
since none of their husbands' jobs in Chinatown offered such insurance. Garment work suited their needs. And so they became the
growing work force of the garment industry.

Since the mid-1960s, 90 percent of the garment factories employing Chinese women have been owned by Chinese; many women
prefer working for Chinese employers, and with Chinese co-workers.

It was logical that in this ethnic environment, special work arrangements developed. For instance, a number of women planned flexible
working hours so they could care for their young children. Sometimes they were permitted to bring children to the factories, and, of
course, location of their workplace within the community was a great
convenience.

For the garment industry the Chinatown situation was ideal. Not
only had it solved its labor force problem but garment manufacturers
could leave factory management to Chinese contractors, who handled
the language problem, worked out wage scales, and even dealt with
the union.

Thus, to understand the development of the Chinatown garment
industry, it is necessary to examine the levels on which it operates.
At the top are the manufacturers, who determine what and how
much to produce; they oversee designing, pattern making; then supply the fabric and provide shipping and cutting facilities. The actual
production is turned over to contractors, the factory owners, who
hire workers to sew the garments. Once the workers produce the
garments, the manufacturers merchandise them to retailers.

The hiring, firing, and management of workers is left to the contractors. When there is a slowdown in consumer buying, the manufacturers simply stop ordering and the contractors absorb the loss.
When workers demand higher wages, it is the contractors they must
confront, although the prices manufacturers pay for the finished
goods dictate the wage scale.

It is not surprising that manufacturers have encouraged Chinese
to get into the industry by helping them to set up factories as contractors. Start-up capital for a garment factory is not high. At today's
prices $25,000 is usually enough to set up a twenty-five to thirty-
person garment shop, complete with a boiler for steam-pressure
machines and the necessary electric and gas hookups from equipment
suppliers.[9] Moreover, the mushrooming of garment factories in
Chinatown has been helped by what economists and the industry
call the "farming out" process. In the 1960s American manufacturers,
equipment suppliers, and other garment-related business firms all

provided Chinese contractors with generous and easy terms to get started: a low down payment of $6,000 to $7,000, with the remainder to be paid in installments over an eighteen-to-twenty-four-month period.

Chinese families with sufficient savings could easily enter the business. Critical for these families, though, was the decision by American manufacturers to shift their production orders to Chinatown. Thus, the industry virtually provided the capital for Chinese owners to start their businesses. The owners, in addition to making a small investment, in effect acted as labor contractors.

Once the Chinese entered the industry, garment factories multiplied in Chinatown. The first two were actually started as early as 1948 by ex-G.I.s, who hired newly arrived Chinese women. In 1960 there were 8 Chinese factories, 34 in 1965, 209 in 1974, and 500 in 1984.

The impact on Chinatown's economy was profound. It has turned Chinatown families into two-income households, stimulating local business. A 1983 study done by the International Ladies Garment Workers Union estimated that the Chinatown garment industry, through wages and profits, put at least $125 million annually into the city's economy: about $32 million was spent in Chinatown.[10] The profits of the Chinese contractors enabled them to expand, as well as to venture into new fields. Many owners of today's large restaurants and import-export companies made their money originally from garment factories.

The rise of the garment industry signaled the transformation of Chinatown from a small service-oriented economy into a community with manufacturing industries. Most importantly, these new industries no longer employ just family members or relatives; they hire dozens, sometimes hundreds of women who are not related. Capital has been concentrated in a few hands, and the polarization of classes in the community has increased.

The development of the garment industry in Chinatown occurred because Chinese women were available just when the industry needed a new source of labor. Once employed, the hardworking women made the accumulation of capital by their employers possible. These profits, when reinvested, stimulated the Chinatown economy to take off and expand.

CHANGING TASTE
BOOSTED CHINESE
RESTAURANT TRADE

The large number of garment factories boosted the local restaurant business. Women working ten to twelve hours a day had little time for housework, child care, and cooking. Many Chinatown restaurants, sensing profits, hung barbecued ducks, chickens, ribs, and other cooked foods in their windows to attract the attention of seamstresses rushing home after work. To simplify their chores, the women would buy these ready-made dishes. Once home, they would put rice in automatic cookers, use their woks to stir-fry vegetables bought fresh from Chinatown street vendors, and prepare the family's dinner.

When I first started as a community worker in the late 1960s, one thing I enjoyed was eating at Chinatown rice shops. My favorite dishes were pickled Chinese vegetables with beef on rice and the famous *san bo fan* ("three treasures rice plate"): pieces of barbecued duck, soy-sauce chicken, and Chinese sausage on top of steamed rice. These individual servings were made even more appealing when the cook put a fried egg and vegetables on top—all for just $1.50! At that price I had no incentive to cook for myself.

That's what garment workers had for lunch as well. They ate at restaurants or, to save time, took meals back to their sewing machines. The restaurants were designed for Chinese who wanted decent, quick, and cheap food. They were small, greasy, simple in the extreme, and always noisy and crowded. To open such a place, one needed little capital. Often cooks and a few waiters pooled their savings. There were dozens of these places in the community.

Before the 1970s, Chinese food was popular with some Americans:

it was reasonably priced and exotic. But its authenticity was eroded by the dictates of American taste. Such things as chop suey, egg foo yung, and chow mein were passed off as traditional dishes. *Chop suey* in Cantonese means literally "miscellaneous pieces"; it is a dish that combines leftovers—something no self-respecting cook would be caught making. *Chow mein* means "fried noodles"—except that the Chinese do not cook anything to the consistency of potato chips and would certainly never consider chow mein a main course. As for *egg foo yung*—"egg" is clearly English; *foo yung* is a Cantonese word indicating the lushness of hibiscus blossoms. *Egg foo yung* means "eggs in full bloom," which tells us very little about the dish. All these names seem almost like jokes, but it's hard to tell whom the joke is on: the chef or the patrons.

Few of the early Chinese who operated restaurants were trained in the trade. They fell into the business because other jobs were not available. The cooking tended to be home-style at best, reflecting the owner's rural Cantonese origins. The food was not of high quality, nor was it imaginative.

Starting in the 1970s, Chinese food became very popular. Americans began to take Chinese cuisine seriously. One may, perhaps, trace this development to Nixon's visit to China, when the American public was given details of the twelve-course state banquets, with spicy Szechuan cooking and mouth-burning Mai-Tai liquor. A "China fever" spread throughout the country.

This new interest in Chinese food, however, is really a reflection of a changing American life style. In New York City in the last twenty years, the life style has been influenced by increasing numbers of high-income professionals, managers, and white-collar workers in corporations and financial institutions. They demand sophisticated services, luxury apartments, designer clothing, fashionable nightclubs, and gourmet restaurants.[11] They soon began to eat out more often and to try different cuisines. When they started looking for new and better-quality food, Chinese restaurant owners recognized the opportunity. In New York, Chinatown has the advantage of being near Wall Street and the municipal office buildings. Office workers ventured into Chinatown for business lunches. In response to the demand, spacious, stylish restaurants were opened, with well-known chefs recruited from Hong Kong and Taiwan preparing the best of Chinese regional dishes: spicy Szechuan and Hunan foods, Peking duck, Cantonese *dim sum*, Shanghai steamed dumplings, and Hong Kong ten-course banquets. As more restaurants opened, each brought innovations, such as the recent emphasis on seafood for the health-conscious American public.

Nixon's visit to China in 1972 was important in a different way. For one thing, it signaled a thaw between two bitter enemies. It became acceptable and even "chic" to be aware of things Chinese. This new attitude toward China added a new dimension to the way Americans related to the Chinese in this country. The Chinese rose in status as American interest in their culture grew. The Chinese, in turn, felt greater pride in their heritage.

The Uptown Chinese attitude toward Chinatown also began to change. Previously, many considered Chinatown a slum and were ashamed of it. As Chinatown began to develop, as the Chinese felt pride in their roots, the Uptown Chinese began to patronize Chinatown shops. They went downtown regularly to try different restaurants, to buy Chinese ingredients, even to see Chinese movies. As a result, they helped to boost the economy of Chinatown. Half a dozen new supermarkets opened to cater to their tastes. *Dim sum* and other dishes are now frozen or canned and sold to those living in the suburbs.

Thus, the development of Chinatown's economy has been spurred by two growth industries—the garment and restaurant trades. This situation is contrary to the general notion that immigrants get jobs in declining industries. Chinese restaurants grew in response to the new American life style. Chinatown garment factories produce to satisfy the world of women's fashions. A significant part of their work is to complete jobs for the "spot market." This market was created for domestic producers because of the inability of foreign importers to meet changing demands for sophisticated and quickly changing women's fashions.

In any event, once the garment and restaurant industries expanded, the foundation was laid for Chinatown's economy to diversify, attracting Chinese of all classes to the community.

WHITE-COLLAR WORKERS AND PROFESSIONALS

With the increasing availability of jobs in Chinatown, more immigrants entered the country. And as the number of people multiplied, the demand for goods and services continued to grow. Most new immigrants, however, do not have the opportunity to learn English, because they start working as soon as they arrive. Thus, 54.8 percent of Chinatown residents speak English poorly or not at all. This does not mean that they are not trying to learn; in fact, there are at least two dozen English-language schools in the community, sponsored by churches, social agencies, and volunteer groups. Thousands of working people squeeze time out from their busy schedules to attend classes. However, the real problem is that they do not have the opportunity to use English on the job or with other Chinese immigrants. They soon forget the scant English they have learned.

The community has developed a number of bilingual services for the non-English-speaking immigrants. Today, a newly arrived immigrant who does not speak English does not have to be concerned. Everything in Chinatown is in Chinese. Banks, the phone company, and hospitals employ Chinese on their staffs. Local service agencies, such as the senior-citizen centers, job-training programs, and mental-health clinics, are Chinese-staffed, and often Chinese-run. Staff members at the bilingual service agencies are usually recruited from Hong Kong and Taiwan, since few Chinese Americans possess adequate command of Chinese.

There is an increasing demand for bilingual professionals. In the mid-1970s, when Chinatown's expansion was in its infancy, professionals were not willing to work in the community because of the low salaries. Now, due to the growing demand, salaries have improved. Some foreign students have decided to work in Chinatown after graduation. Even some second-generation professionals have settled there to work in the community. In 1973 Chinatown had only twelve lawyers; in 1986, there were approximately seventy-two.

The local Chinese-language newspapers have been able to recruit experienced reporters and editors from Hong Kong, Taiwan, and the People's Republic. These individuals have generally a poor command of English and would have had no chance of earning a living prior to the transformation of the Chinatown economy. Today, their positions are sought by many, even by a few Chinese trained in American journalism schools. These newspaper professionals have brought the former cut-and-paste news operations to the standards of journalism practiced in Hong Kong and Taiwan.

There are nine local Chinese daily newspapers in New York. In them one finds pages of advertisements for professional services of all types: Chinese-speaking lawyers, doctors, tax accountants, stock and investment consultants, realtors, travel agents. The 1984 *Chinatown Business Directory* listed seventy-eight doctors, including many specializing in traditional medicine: acupuncturists, bone and joint healers, herbalists (who prescribe awful-tasting medicinal drinks intended to enhance one's spirit, energy, or virility), and specialists in "operationless" treatment of hemorrhoids—a common occupational disease in Chinatown. There were also fifty-one accounting firms and eleven Chinese-managed stock-brokerage firms.[12]

DYNAMIC CONSUMER INDUSTRIES

As Chinatown's population grew, opportunities for a variety of small-scale businesses opened up. Instead of working in sewing factories and restaurants, some immigrants started retail businesses with very little capital; they worked long hours for marginal profits.

They often shared space with others; some even began as street vendors. On weekends and during the daily rush hours, Chinatown streets became packed with vendors selling newspapers, vegetables, fish, and fruits. Now, because of very high rents, radios, watches, jewelry, clothing, shoes, and snack foods are sold right on the sidewalks.

The common impression of outsiders is that Chinatown's economy depends on the tourists in souvenir shops and chop-suey restaurants. Today, however, the community's main businesses are those patronized by resident Chinese. Due to keen competition, businesses, in order to survive, sell high-quality goods at reasonable prices; above all, they must satisfy the needs and tastes of their Chinese customers.

Businesses are surprisingly varied: taxi services by Chinese drivers on twenty-four-hour call; Chinese-speaking Honda and Buick dealers; auto driving schools which guarantee that their students with a minimum knowledge of English will be able to pass the written and road tests to get a license.

Real estate is one of the most important businesses; there are more than fifty Chinese real-estate agencies dealing with the renting, buying, and selling of factory lofts, storefronts, office and apartment buildings in Chinatown, or restaurants in the suburbs. To the upwardly mobile Chinese, they offer houses in Queens and Long Island, or even condominiums in Chinese-owned and -managed retirement villages in Orlando, Florida.

Chinatown caters to Chinese taste. There are now some 450 large and small restaurants, with a new one opening every week. Originally, there were only Cantonese and a few second-rate Szechuan restaurants. Today, the choice is wide: you can have Fukien and Soochow food, or the popular spicy Chowchou cuisine, which originated with the Hakka ("guest people") in Kwangtung. The diner may also order a Taiwanese version of the Mongolian hot pot or easily find a quick and inexpensive meal of Hong Kong wonton, Shanghai dumplings, or Cantonese noodles. Then there are the ethnic Chinese Thai, Vietnamese, and Burmese restaurants. A couple of Hong Kong–style "nouvelle cuisine" restaurants have recently opened. There are even Chinese-run Western and Japanese restaurants serving "foreign" food modified to Chinese taste.

New businesses thrive because they are able to make the life of the immigrant easier. Aside from the Chinese daily newspapers, there are two weekly and three monthly magazines, all published locally. Most report news from the Far East, though increasingly they cover both American and Chinatown developments. Seven Chinese movie theaters show films, mainly from Hong Kong and Taiwan—the selection is not ideal: half the movies are the kung-fu variety; most of the rest are melodramatic love stories or farces. There are two Chinese direct-wire subscription radio stations, four TV production companies which rent air time from different commercial stations (mostly rebroadcasting Hong Kong and Taiwan TV programs), two amateur Cantonese opera troupes, and periodic visits by professional troupes from Taiwan. A multitude of videocassette rental shops provide Chinese "soap operas," martial arts, or soft-core pornographic tapes produced in Hong Kong and Taiwan.

Chinatown has developed into a vital consumer center. Half a dozen supermarkets supply practically everything one can find in Taiwan, Hong Kong, or the People's Republic of China. These businesses cater to the taste and habits of their community and thus help to preserve its distinctive Chinese culture. Many immigrants may not consciously intend to maintain their tradition and customs, but the shops constantly remind them of their heritage: in September they sell moon cakes to celebrate the Mid-Autumn Festival; in February, rice cakes for the Chinese New Year.

CHINESE FROM ALL
PARTS OF THE WORLD

Rapid development in Chinatown has provided a wide variety of opportunities. It is no wonder that more and more immigrants are attracted to it.

New York Chinatown's population before the 1970s consisted

only of immigrants from Kwangtung and Hong Kong, but since then it has drawn Cantonese-speaking people from around the world. At the end of the Vietnam War thousands of Vietnamese, Laotian, and Cambodian refugees of Chinese descent, who spoke Chinese and originally came from Kwangtung, came to Chinatown. Cantonese-speaking Chinese from Burma, Malaysia, Indonesia, Jamaica, Cuba, Brazil, and many other Third World countries also found their way to New York. The Fukienese, another major overseas Chinese group, many of whom were sailors, have followed the Cantonese to this country.

It seems that these new immigrants, who had wandered to different parts of the world to escape poverty and civil wars in China, found their original refuge unsatisfactory. They came to settle in Chinatowns across the United States.

In this respect, New York's Chinatown is somewhat different from those of other cities. Because of its large pool of manual labor and service jobs, New York's Chinatown tends to pre-select immigrants of working-class origin much more than other American Chinatowns. Chinese with professional and technical skills prefer California or Hawaii, where there are already established communities of Chinese professionals. Thus, in 1979, according to an Immigration and Naturalization Service study, among all Chinese who came to the United States, 14.6 percent were professional or technical workers, but only 3.2 percent of them intended to settle in New York.[13] New York's Chinatown is attracting poorer, less skilled, and less educated immigrants than other Chinatowns.

Once the expansion of Chinatown began, Mandarin-speaking people from Taiwan began to settle on the fringes, especially after 1976, when the Taiwanese government liberalized exit requirements. After 1979, Chinese from the People's Republic were allowed to emigrate directly to this country. They came from all parts of China and were unprepared to deal with the American capitalistic, competitive system; they, more than any other group, needed Chinatown.

New York's Chinatown has become the gathering place for Chinese from all parts of the world. They bring their specialized trades and distinctive tastes with them. Groups with different dialects, who cannot understand one another, concentrate in separate sections of Chinatown: Fukienese on Division Street, Burmese Chinese on Henry Street, Chinese from Taiwan on Centre Street, Vietnamese on East Broadway.

A complex community has taken shape in New York. Newcomers with diverse backgrounds have joined the community, gradually creating a previously nonexistent middle class of white-collar workers, professionals, sales personnel, and vendors. At the same time, the economy has diversified from small-scale service operations into the manufacturing, wholesale, consumer, professional, and entertainment trades.

New York's Chinatown (and other American Chinatowns) is unlike the traditional European immigrant ghetto, where residents remained only until they found better jobs and began integrating into American society. The Chinese concentrate in Chinatown because there are jobs right in the community.

S O F A R, I have dealt only briefly with the role of foreign capital from the Far East in Chinatown's development. I want to emphasize, however, that the influx of capital was not the main reason for Chinatown's economic growth. In fact, foreign capital did not play a role in the beginning; it was the dramatic increase of Chinese garment and restaurant industries that opened up new economic frontiers, and set the stage for economic boom in the 1970s. Only after the expansion of these two businesses did foreign investment pour in.

Without the promise of growth, foreign capital had no reason to come to Chinatown. The former stagnant business climate offered little incentive. In fact, since the 1950s, Taiwan and Hong Kong have industrialized rapidly and become highly developed consumer economies absorbing capital that otherwise might have come to Chinatown. However, once it became clear that the economies of American Chinatowns were growing, Far East businessmen saw opportunities. Some of the new garment-factory owners had worked in Hong Kong firms, producing garments for export to America under contract to American manufacturers. Others opened restaurants, copying successful operations in Hong Kong. The skill and know-how of these small investors had more impact on Chinatown than the amount of capital they brought with them.

Imported capital, invested in the United States, took advantage of immigrant labor in Chinatown and reaped high profits. These profits attracted even more investments. More investments created more jobs, encouraging more immigration. This, in turn, brought more profits. This cycle generated the economic boom in Chinatown of the 1970s.

Thus, while foreign capital was not the *cause* of Chinatown's economic expansion, it did stimulate it. However, by the late 1970s, the character of foreign capital from the Far East began to change. And, as we shall see, the impact of growing foreign investments undermined the very foundation of Chinatown society.

The Woes
of Foreign
Capital

3

FOREIGN CAPITAL is a dirty phrase around New York's Chinatown. It is blamed for all ills. Many people believe that much of it goes into speculating in Chinatown real estate and has caused the value of land to skyrocket. Rents have been jacked up for restaurants, garment factories, grocery stores, and residences, to the point of forcing many to relocate to Queens and Brooklyn.

PRODUCTIVE FOREIGN CAPITAL

In the early 1970s, foreign investments tended to be small, usually made by businessmen who sold their operations in Hong Kong and brought small amounts of capital to New York. Once established in Chinatown, they worked hard, took advantage of free family labor, squeezed as much as possible out of their Chinese employees, pinched every penny, and even cheated on taxes. Theirs was considered "productive capital," its purpose and scope being in line with realistic expectations of returns. Most community people believe that such foreign investments have been helpful in creating jobs.

In the mid-1970s, the pace of foreign investment began to accelerate. Two major fears brought a flood of capital into Chinatown. First was the uncertain political climate in the Far East created by the withdrawal of the American forces in Vietnam; there was a strong fear of imminent communist dominance in the region. People in Hong Kong were also concerned about the status of the British Crown Colony after 1997, when the lease of the New Territories would end. Many expected that China would reclaim the colony and eliminate its system of free enterprise. Many Taiwanese also feared for their island's future after the United States became increasingly friendly to the People's Republic. Since most Asian countries experienced a period of rapid growth in the 1950s and 1960s, many Chinese in Hong Kong, Taiwan, and Macao, as well as the ethnic Chinese in Malaysia, Indonesia, Thailand, Burma, and the Philippines, made a great deal of money. However, political uncertainty caused them to look to the United States to shelter their fortunes. Chinese communities in this country seemed in the 1970s to be ideal for this purpose.

The second major factor influencing the movement of foreign capital into the United States was the world recession that followed the 1973 energy crisis. Most countries suffered economic depression coupled with high inflation. The United States, the center of the capitalist world economy, fared better than most. A large volume of foreign capital flowed into the country to earn the high interest rates offered by American banks. Chinese capital was part of this movement.

The volume of this capital—and its political implication—cannot be overestimated. A large number of people in Hong Kong and Taiwan began to transfer their capital as the first step in the decision to leave their homeland. They turned to North America, Australia, Britain, and Singapore as places for resettlement.

The transfer of capital preceded their physical move. It was not simply the rich but thousands of middle-class professional and businessmen who shifted their money. While the rich moved part of their business operations to the United States, the less wealthy put their savings in the care of relatives, who made deposits in Chinatown banks to avoid complicated rules governing non-residents. Many banks were set up precisely to facilitate such transactions—they were not strict about client identification and income-tax and banking regulations. Thus, Chinatown residents of very modest means may have tens of thousands of dollars in CD accounts at the local banks. When the Golden Pacific Bank was declared insolvent in 1985, federal regulators who examined the books found hundreds of Chinese-held savings accounts over $20,000;[1] there were 170 accounts with more than the federally insured maximum of $100,000.[2] Chinese newspaper reporters speculated that many of these individuals were simply holding large sums of money on behalf of friends and relatives in the Far East.

Overseas Chinese have also transferred money to the United States by investing it in their relations' businesses or real-estate ventures. The total of all these small investors' capital has given a tremendous boost to the Chinatown economy. In addition, some Chinatown banks are suspected of being involved in the "laundering" of illegal income from drug operations in the Far East.[3]

Around 1978, at the time of negotiations between Great Britain and China on the future of Hong Kong, and about the time when the United States recognized the People's Republic as the legitimate government of China, political uncertainty greatly destabilized the currency values and stock markets in both Hong Kong and Taiwan. The exodus of capital drastically increased the flow of investments into New York's Chinatown.

The extent of this increase is suggested by the number of banks that opened in New York's Chinatown. In the 1940s there were only two banks: an American bank, the Coin Exchange (the forerunner of Chemical Bank), and the Bank of China, which was the official Nationalist Chinese bank, dealing mainly with dollar remittances to China. The Manhattan Bank and the North American Bank were opened in the late 1960s. Only in the mid-1970s did larger banks, like Chase Manhattan, Citibank, and Franklin Savings, open branches. In the 1980s, with the deregulation of banking rules, banks literally flooded Chinatown. By 1986, there were twenty-seven banks in the community: about one-third were branches of American banks, and the rest were Chinese-owned. From 1981 to 1986, fourteen Chinese-owned banks opened.[4] Assets of these banks, estimated to be over $2 billion in reserve, came mainly from Hong Kong and Taiwan, with the rest from Southeast Asian countries.

Part of the banking activities is concerned with import ventures. Importers from Hong Kong, the People's Republic, and Taiwan, attracted by the growth of Chinatown, have financed the construction of supermarkets and department stores to supply dry goods, canned foods, clothing, and other consumer needs. With the rapid development of industries and the advancement of technology, the balance of Pacific Rim trade within the last twenty years has shifted increasingly in favor of the Far East. Exporters from this region are pushing a variety of expensive items, including designer clothing, electronic goods, antiques, audio equipment, and even personal computers. Chinatown, in the meantime, has been used as a testing ground for American consumers, as well as a beachhead for expansion into American markets. Wholesale distribution centers, dealerships, and import branch offices have crowded into the community.

INVESTMENT BEHAVIOR OF FOREIGN CAPITAL

Foreign investment in import ventures represents only part of the capital flow. Much of the foreign capital investments from the Far East which came to this country after the late 1970s behave differently from ordinary capital. Maximization of profits is usually not the primary objective of these investors. More important is the trade-off between possible high returns and low-risk investment. A number of Chinese investors are also trying to escape the uncertain political climate in the Far East. To do so, they devise investment strategies to gain U.S. immigration status.

Taiwan, for example, maintains tight control over the exit of both capital and people. Owners of Taiwanese companies circumvent these laws by setting up branch offices in the United States. Such offices can send the owners or their relatives to the United States as branch officers, who can then legally move capital out of Taiwan. The officers of firms registered in the United States can apply for, and obtain, immigration status. Once this has been done, the new branch officers may travel between the United States and Taiwan without restriction, and their relatives in Taiwan may apply for immigrant status as well. In the end, the owners, their families, and their capital can move out of Taiwan whenever they choose. It is also very common to find a Chinese business family residing in two places: a husband with a green card (U.S. permanent residency status) working in Taiwan or Hong Kong and commuting to visit his family in the United States, where his children can get a better education. In such cases, the transfer of capital is used to help the immigration process.

Chinese money from the Far East flows only one way; the intention is to move capital to the United States. Profits are not returned to Asia but are reinvested in this country.

The objective is to sacrifice short-term profits for long-term growth and stability. This long-term view accepts a lower rate of return than would commonly be expected of ordinary American capital. In fact, some investors are willing to make no profit at all, and even to suffer losses for a few years, as long as they can maintain a secure financial position in this country. This last feature plays havoc with the normally competitive Chinatown economy. Many clothing stores, restaurants, and other businesses hardly have any business, yet they all continue to operate, forcing other firms to engage in suicidal competition and even driving some out of business altogether.

Adding more confusion to this economic climate is the competition between Taiwan and the People's Republic to woo the support of the Chinese in America. To counter the effects of the increasingly friendly relationship between Washington and Peking, the Taiwan government invested capital in New York's Chinatown in order to maintain its political hold on the community. It bought a number of important real-estate holdings and set up department stores, travel bureaus, and trade exhibition centers. Government officials have awarded lucrative franchises, business contracts, and favorable import concessions to those who are loyal to their cause. These investments are to achieve political objectives; they are not subject to the law of supply-and-demand, and those who benefit do so regardless of public need or the quality of service.

Officials of the People's Republic, on the other hand, are pouring capital into Chinatown, with the goal of replacing Taiwan's dominance. Also, the investments are part of its "united front" strategy to isolate Taiwan and to pressure it to agree to peaceful unification.

Their most heated competition is on the media front. This war has been fought mainly in New York's Chinatown. Both governments relocated their worldwide propaganda centers for overseas Chinese from Hong Kong to New York, which is recognized as the communication center of the world. In the late 1970s, each side expanded its propaganda machine, buying out small daily newspapers and television stations, setting up modern satellite transmission systems, hiring hundreds of highly qualified reporters, establishing news bureaus, and publishing local editions in major cities across the country. Editorials and news items are distributed to smaller Chinese newspapers worldwide through international networks.

REAL ESTATE AND
CHINATOWN GROWTH

Foreign investors looking for low-risk ventures generally prefer non-liquid assets: real estate provides this type of investment. It requires less attention than liquid assets, its value is not likely to depreciate, and it is a valuable asset if the owners decide to relocate to this country. It is not surprising that more and more foreign capital has flowed into real estate.[5]

Ownership of land has always been important to the Chinese. It represents stability and power. Every association in Chinatown has to have its own headquarters building, and all tongs define their influence in territorial terms. In rapidly expanding Chinatown there has been a crying need for space: space for stores, factories, wholesale storage, offices, and, most of all, for housing the new immigrants.

One important factor was vital to the recent growth of Chinatown—the availability of land during its period of expansion. The influx of Chinese began in the late 1960s, while New York City was in decline: manufacturing industries and corporate headquarters were moving out, causing a steady loss of jobs. Consequently, New Yorkers moved away. In 1974 the city almost went bankrupt, partly because of the loss of income from taxes. Neighborhoods on the Lower East Side of Manhattan, and especially areas surrounding old Chinatown, were in decay. Factories, offices, warehouses, and storefronts were abandoned or underutilized. Old tenement houses, built in the last century for Jewish and Italian immigrants, were in disrepair because the former residents had long since moved away. These buildings provided space for the new Chinese immigrants at a relatively affordable cost.

Chinese landlords and groups of investors gradually bought the old buildings. Chinatown began to move into surrounding neighborhoods: north into Little Italy, leaving only small pockets of Italian restaurants, cafés, and elderly residents; east into the half-deserted old Jewish neighborhood—with some of its most famous immigrant landmarks, like the *Jewish Daily Forward* building—and even into parts of the Orchard Street market; south to City Hall and the court buildings; and west beyond Broadway to SoHo, which was in the process of becoming a community of artists, chic galleries, restaurants, and shops.

The area of expansion was very large. Most people have the impression that Chinatown housing is expensive because there is a shortage of buildings. This is only partly true; the high cost of renovating the century-old buildings pushed up the price of housing. When a Chinese landlord acquired a building and didn't have the capital to renovate it, he would wait until demand for the housing became so great that he could charge high rents. Then he would proceed with renovations.

Chinatown since the late sixties has been a classic case of community development through the hard work of the people, who created the condition for real-estate owners to make high profits. The owners speculated in real estate and pushed the prices well beyond the reach of residents. This eventually undermined the community economy.

SPECULATIVE CAPITAL AND THE COMMUNITY

A few years ago any thoughtful observer could predict that Chinatown would continue to expand rapidly. When the United States normalized relations with the People's Republic of China in 1979 and the government increased the Chinese immigration quota from 20,600 to 40,600 a year, there would be more Chinese coming and seeking living quarters. An investor in Chinatown real estate could double his investment in two or three years. For instance, I lived in an old, dilapidated warehouse building on East Broadway for eleven years. When I first moved there in 1973, the rent was $140 a month for a 2,000-square-foot loft. In 1975 the Jewish owner sold the five-story building to a Hong Kong developer for $270,000. In 1984 the new owner forced all the tenants out and put the building up for sale for $3 million.

This situation has encouraged real-estate dealers to buy buildings, with no intention of improving them. They hold them only long enough to sell them at much higher prices. The next owner does the same thing. This practice is familiar to most Chinese from Hong Kong, where it's called "frying the real estate in a wok": property gets hotter and hotter. There is a lot more money to be made, but the stakes get larger and larger, until only well-financed players have the money to continue. A number of very large Hong Kong developers, veterans in this game, moved part of their operations to New York. Today, several such firms own hundreds of buildings in the community.

The price of buildings has leaped out of proportion to the rental income. As this process continues, landlords will continue to jack up rents. New York City has no rent control on commercial buildings, and once the leases came up for renewal, some Chinese landlords increased rents by 200 to 300 percent. What is worse, the landlords did not give long leases. Thus, businessmen face increasing uncertainties.

Retail space has become so scarce that unusual situations have developed: newspaper stands are located underneath a building staircase; souvenir vendors rent sidewalk space from store owners and use a basement hatch door opening as behind-the-counter space; a small store has fish for sale on one side and radios on the other. Merchants pay dearly for the use of such space. One vegetable seller on Canal Street rents a 150-square-foot storefront, which he uses only for storage, and displays his produce on stands set up on the street. He pays $1,500 a month for the storefront, having also paid $20,000 as "key money" to the landlord. A number of smaller businesses have simply been forced to close.

The desire of Chinese retailers to locate in the heart of Chinatown is so strong that they are paying unbelievable prices. According to a study done by the Real Estate Board of New York, the annual rent per square foot for retail space on Canal Street is $275. That is higher than rents on Madison Avenue above Forty-second Street ($255), and higher than the most desirable parts of the Upper West Side, and it is far higher than on Wall Street, where the rents are around $175 per square foot.[6]

Compounding the problem is the rejuvenation of New York City. Real estate, particularly in Manhattan, is going through what is called the "gentrification" process: poorer neighborhoods are being converted to high-rise and condominium communities. The same pattern is occurring in Chinatown. As the gap between the prices of buildings and the real income from them increases, landlords are no longer content with just getting tenants who will pay higher rents. It is even more profitable to convert old commercial and industrial buildings into office use. On East Broadway alone, at least ten garment factories closed down between 1983 and 1986 because their buildings were converted for use as offices. In fact, East Broadway is now known as the "Wall Street of Chinatown"[7]: five new banks have opened on the street since the factories closed.

For real-estate interests to take full advantage of this speculative fever, they need to displace low-income residents from the existing standard, five-story, rent-controlled tenements where most of Chinatown's working people live. The profits from such conversions are so tempting that some landlords use unethical means to drive tenants out. The most notorious case concerns the East-West Tower on Henry Street. A development corporation, reputed to be financed by the Burmese ethnic Chinese, applied to the City Community Board for a special zoning permit to build a 33-story residential apartment complex on a plot occupied by several rent-controlled tenements. The new building was intended for upper-middle-income residents willing to pay a minimum $150,000 for an apartment (at 1982 values). A permit was granted to the Overseas Chinese Corporation after a formal hearing before the Community Board in the fall of 1981. By then the developer had already evicted the tenants and demolished the buildings. The former residents filed a suit against the development corporation, charging it with harassment, gang intimidation, arson, and deprivation of basic services to force them out—even before it had been granted the city permit. The New York City Department of Investigation inquired into and confirmed the tenants' charges.[8] Their report generated enough opposition in the community to force the Community Board to revoke the permit.

Since then, several attempts have been made to win approval of other high-rise condominiums. Developers claim that there is a great shortage of housing in the community. But with the present cuts in federal assistance for low-income housing, developments are much more likely to be for upper-income families. Furthermore, builders point out that there are more than enough Chinese tenants willing to pay high rents.[9] This may very well be true—condominiums in Chinatown are ideal for overseas investors. The value will appreciate, the space can be rented, relatives can live in them, and, in some cases, children of the owner can live in them while going to American colleges.

The very prospect of these housing changes has destabilized the community. No one is certain about the future. People do not know whether they will be able to afford to stay in Chinatown.

CHINATOWN ECONOMY IN THE 1980s

Higher rents have reduced the profits of restaurants, factories, and other businesses. Higher rents have cut deeply into workers' already low wages. Businesses have cut staff and increased the work load of the remaining work force. Workers are faced with frequent layoffs; they are overworked, underpaid, or underemployed. Without steady income, their consumer power has been reduced. If this trend continues, the garment factories will disappear and thousands of residents will lose a major source of income. Restaurants, groceries, and other businesses dependent on factory workers will also close. The economy of the community will collapse. Real-estate speculators and banks will have killed the goose that laid the golden egg.

Still, real estate continues to attract a larger and larger share of investments which previously went into industry. New banks have been established to take advantage of this situation. With deposits of foreign capital, they move aggressively into land acquisitions and offer credit to developers and speculators.

On the other hand, loans for restaurants and garment factories are harder to get, since they are considered high-risk ventures. In fact, those who have made money in garment and restaurant businesses are now moving money into real estate. This exodus of capital has created a situation where only the large enterprises can survive. Thus there is a concentration of capital in the community economy; fewer and fewer individuals own more and more businesses.

While most of the community is aware of the seriousness of the housing problem, few agree on solutions. There are those who feel that further gentrification is inevitable; it has happened elsewhere. Chinatown residents from Hong Kong certainly experienced it before they emigrated. According to their viewpoint, Chinatown simply has to cope with the situation. Officials of the Chinatown Planning Council advocate the decentralization of Chinatown into satellite communities in the outer boroughs of Queens and Brooklyn. They argue that factories and residents should move out so that Manhattan's Chinatown can be developed into an upscale business area.

An estimated 40 percent of Chinatown workers already live outside the area. Pockets of Chinese concentrations have emerged along the various subway lines leading to Chinatown. The largest is in Queens. The main street in Flushing is lined with supermarkets, grocery stores, and restaurants, owned mainly by Chinese from Taiwan, and some garment factories have moved to Long Island City.

This process of decentralization, aside from the tremendous hardship involved for those relocating, means that Chinatown will never be the same. That's why some people in the community oppose the dispersal. As they see it, real-estate interests and speculative capital should not be allowed to destroy people's homes and livelihoods. Several activist groups are working to counter this process. The Asian American Legal Defense and Education Fund took action to block a high-rise, high-rent development on Henry Street, because it would have a damaging environmental impact on the community. It won the case.

The real-estate business in Chinatown is highly competitive. Speculators have the financial power and political leverage to get what they want. And they know what they want, because they have spent time and energy analyzing the community. It is difficult for ordinary residents, especially recent immigrants, successfully to confront such a powerful interest group.

Most land-use experts, who have observed the transformation of other parts of Manhattan, are not optimistic about saving Chinatown, particularly because it is so close to Wall Street and all the major transportation arteries. Also, as 1997 approaches, the pressures will increase as more immigrants and capital flow in from Hong Kong.

However, there are several unique factors that might spare Chinatown from destruction. The core area—Mott, Pell, Mulberry, and Bayard Streets—is owned by Chinese associations. So far, they have not been involved in real-estate speculation, partly because members of these groups cannot agree on a common plan. Second, a large section of Chinatown consists of hundreds of units of rent-controlled tenement housing. Gentrification of these buildings is difficult, because they are fully occupied. The only possible targets are the less than a dozen empty lots which are too small for high-rises. If the existing tenements are protected and zoning restrictions are maintained, it will not be possible to displace the present residents. The areas subject to intense speculation are loft buildings on streets outside the core area. That's where new businesses are competing for space and where rents have reached unbelievable heights. With speculation getting out of hand, land values will eventually fall to their real worth. The price will be determined by the real economic activities of the community. Prices can continue to rise only if there are new customers willing to pay higher prices. But Chinatown buildings are appealing only to Chinese businesses. Non-Chinese firms will find the prices too high and the space utilization peculiar to the Chinese. So if the existing businesses cannot afford to pay the rents, the buildings will become vacant. In the last five years there has been a rash of conversions of factory lofts to office space; now that there is a glut, the per/foot value has fallen.[10] There has also been a rash of conversions of storefronts into mini shopping malls, where dozens of retailers share one subdivided space. In 1987 there are too many of these.

In the meantime, other market forces will affect land speculation in Chinatown: factory owners will move uptown and large real-estate investors will switch their money into non-Chinatown properties— less money for more returns.

The present situation offers a real opportunity to form a community coalition to block gentrification. As the housing situation deteriorates, the general lines of the conflict are becoming clear, cutting to the very heart of the community problem. The community is objectively split: landlords, banks, real-estate dealers, and foreign investors versus the "productive" business interests, individual workers, residents, and some traditional associations. A united front could be formed by the latter groups around a very specific strategy focusing on maintaining rent-control laws, fighting the violation of tenants' rights, restricting zoning changes, and advocating development of low-income public housing. In the meantime, several groups in Chinatown are already forming political alliances with other Lower East Side black, Puerto Rican, church, and tenants' groups to block gentrification of the old working-class neighborhood. Others are organizing around the concept of "community control" by bringing political pressure on the city's housing-related agencies and by joining community boards in order to promote policies against the speculative fever in Chinatown.

In any event, foreign capital has pushed the community economy to a new stage. From a self-employing, small-business community, New York's Chinatown experienced a period of rapid growth in manufacturing and consumer industries in the 1970s, through capital accumulation based on the labor of women garment workers. Then, in the early 1980s, the economy moved into high finance and real-estate speculation, because of the profitability of landholdings and the influx of foreign capital. But unrestrained foreign investments have led to rising rents, inflated property values, and a shortage of investments in productive businesses. Thus, the economy of Chinatown has slowed down. Two bank runs in Chinatown during 1985 seem to have brought it to a new stage.

A MODEL
MINORITY
COMMUNITY?

4

THERE have been a number of success stories in China-town—immigrants who have become millionaires. Several real-estate giants started out as small, family-run restaurant owners. However, in most instances, Chinatown millionaires are either individuals who have been here since the 1960s or wealthy Hong Kong immigrants who had money before they came. Very few new immigrants who came in the 1970s have prospered. Success is difficult in today's large-scale economy, where capital is concentrated, rents and real-estate values are high, and competition is vicious. One is reminded of a Chinese saying: "For the fame of one general, ten thousand corpses are left on the battlefield." The success of one businessman depends on the exploitation of many immigrants under him.

But the image of widespread success persists. The notion began with the publication of the 1970 Census. It made available for the first time significant statistics on the Chinese in America. The general public was surprised to learn that the Chinese had a higher education level and a higher percentage in professional fields than the national average. What was believed most impressive was the short period of time it took to attain these accomplishments. Thus, Chinese Americans have emerged as a "model minority."

The discovery of this model has reaffirmed the effectiveness of the American melting pot and its application to a nonwhite minority. This has been particularly appealing to conservatives who promote free enterprise and limited government. The sociologist Nathan Glazer has even questioned whether the Chinese, because of their achievements, qualify for affirmative-action programs. Others, like black economist Thomas Sowell, have argued that since the Chinese have succeeded without public assistance, other minorities should not be given preferential treatment, lest they lose the incentive to succeed on their own. Unfortunately, to identify the Chinese as a model minority is to ignore the complex diversity of Chinese communities. To project the Chinese as a model is also a disservice to other minorities and misrepresents the facts.

This ignorance is understandable. For most of American history, the Chinese have been numerically insignificant; for more than a century, their communities existed as isolated entities within cities. As a result, general knowledge of the Chinese was spotty and often contradictory. On one hand, the Chinese were considered to be docile, law-abiding, hardworking, steeped in Confucian traditions (whatever that means). This was the world of Charlie Chan, as portrayed by film star Warner Oland. On the other hand, there was also a sinister association of the Chinese with drugs, gambling, and tong wars. Today, with the dramatic increase through immigration, new impressions of the Chinese in America are superimposed on the old stereotypes, conjuring up a most confusing picture indeed.

The first step in untangling this confusion is to recall the distinction between the Downtown and the Uptown Chinese. These two groups are quite distinct, according to the 1980 Census. The Downtown Chinese, who reside in New York's Chinatown, have much lower median household incomes, a high percentage of people below the poverty level (24.7 percent compared to 17.2 percent for New York City overall),[1] and an exceptionally high percentage of people with-

out high-school diplomas (71.4 percent).[2] These Chinese rarely come
into contact with other groups, except, possibly, in Chinatown restaurants. The Uptown Chinese, in contrast, are a model minority—
educated, well off, and professionally trained.

THE UPTOWN CHINESE

During the years of the Chinese exclusion (1882–1943), as
we have seen, very few Chinese from elite classes stayed in this
country. Scholars who came to attend graduate schools returned
home as soon as their education was completed. There were no
Chinese communities outside Chinatowns.

In 1949 a socialist revolution took place in China. The United
States backed the defeated regime of Generalissimo Chiang Kai-shek
and proceeded to admit refugees from the mainland. Based on the
McCarran-Walter Immigration and Nationality Act of 1952, the
United States admitted some 30,000 Chinese, who were given immigrant status. Included in this group were 5,000 stranded scholars
who had been studying at American universities in 1949 and did
not want to return to China.

The refugees included many of the Chinese elite: young scholars,
former government officials, top financial managers, diplomats, and
generals. They were economically well off and resourceful. As for
the students, almost all of them were attending graduate schools or
research institutes. After 1949 they were no longer supported by
funds from China; the U.S. government stepped in, providing emergency assistance and permitting them to get jobs after graduation.
They were the cream of the Chinese educational establishment. In
staying, they had to downgrade their aspirations, but most were
eventually able to find professional jobs, for they had had a superb
education even by American standards. The distinguished nature of
these stranded scholars should not be underestimated. Some of our
most prominent Chinese Americans come from this group. Among
them are two Nobel Prize winners in physics, Yang Chen Ning and

Lee Tsung Dao; the architect I. M. Pei; An Wang, the founder and
owner of Wang Laboratories; the Wall Street financier of the Manhattan Fund and now president of the American Can Company,
Jerry Tsai. Well educated and skilled in the English language, they
had little trouble in the American job market. Their upbringing
enabled them to be at ease in the American middle class. Nevertheless,
they still experienced discrimination. According to a 1980 United
States Commission on Civil Rights report, the Uptown Chinese
earned less than whites with equivalent levels of education and similar
professional positions,[3] and qualified Chinese are regularly bypassed
for promotions to management positions.[4]

The number of Uptown Chinese slowly increased as second and
third generations of the Downtown Chinese left Chinatowns, aban-
doning their parents' businesses for professional careers.

THE UPTOWN CHINESE
FROM TAIWAN

Then came the Immigration Act of 1965. While the "Uniting
the Family" provision increased the number of immigrants into
Chinatowns, the law also increased the number of Uptown Chinese
under the provision for admitting "needed professional and skilled
persons." The latter provision reflected an awareness that the United
States was no longer a growing industrial economy and did not need
more manual laborers. This was also the time of the intense arms
race with the Soviet Union. The United States invested heavily in
scientific education and training. The change in immigration policy
to admit foreign-trained professionals was seen as part of that process. Students from Taiwan fitted neatly into this scheme.

Between the mid-1960s and the mid-1980s, close to 150,000
Taiwanese students came to the United States for graduate education.
Today they are the largest single group of foreign students studying
in America.[5] Some 97 percent have remained here after graduation
by converting their F–1 student status into immigrant status. This

is easily done when a student finds a job and is sponsored by his employer under the Third Professional Preferential Quota. These student immigrants represent a large proportion of the Uptown Chinese, and they have had the most significant impact on the reputation of the Chinese community in this country.

· Taiwan is a small island with a dense population. It has a highly competitive education system with an elaborate examination structure, similar to that of imperial China. Starting at a very early age, youth are taught that their future depends on their ability to pass examinations and get into good schools: from elementary to junior high to high school, and on to college. At each step, fewer move up. In order to succeed, one has to study hard. Well-to-do families hire private tutors for their children. The social pressure for achievement is so intense that failure brings shame to the whole family. Traditionally, the reward was a position in the government; today, it's the opportunity to take still another examination in order to go to the United States to earn a graduate degree. If the student who passes that exam (part of the exam is English comprehension) is over twenty-one years of age, has served in the army (for males), has been accepted by an American graduate school, and has financial resources (either self-financing or scholarships), he (or she) may leave Taiwan.

Students in Taiwan are taught English beginning in junior high school, and the system encourages them to specialize in fields needed in the American job market. The best students are pushed by teachers and parents into math, physics, or engineering, even if they are more talented and interested in literature or the social sciences. Taiwan tailors its curriculum to the American system, so that its graduates can easily adjust to American graduate schools. It trains its best students for "export." Thus some 70 to 80 percent of science graduates at Taiwan University (the best in Taiwan) leave for America. These students come up to the highest international standards in their fields.

When these highly trained Chinese finish their master's or Ph.D. degrees in American universities, they possess credentials that enable them to start at the top of their professions. Taiwan's elite, partic-

ularly those originally from the Chinese mainland who have dominated the island politically, push their children to settle permanently
in the United States; there is hardly a single high official who does
not have offspring in this country—a classic example of the brain
drain.

These Uptown Chinese of Taiwanese origin possessed a first-class
education before they came to the United States. They were able to
move into relatively high-income professional careers after further
study here. They did not start from scratch. To suggest that they
made it by quickly moving upward misrepresents the facts.

The Taiwan students have joined the political refugees and stranded
scholars of the 1950s to form today's Uptown Chinese. It is they
who have had such a strong influence on the census statistics concerning education, income, and professions. The figures would be
even more impressive had they not included the Downtown Chinese.
In other words, the Chinese population in this country is polarized.
By focusing on averages for the Chinese, the census figures obscure
the real situation.

CHINATOWN: A NEW
OPTION FOR MOBILITY?

Even if one leaves the Uptown Chinese out of the picture,
there are still many who believe that Chinatown is a model of success.
According to this view, the Chinese through hard work and ethnic
solidarity have been able to build a dynamic economy in our contemporary Chinatowns that provides jobs for new immigrants and
the climate for upward mobility.

Most new immigrants are working people; the choices available
to them are limited. Labor economists have divided the American
labor market into two segments. The primary sector includes those
working for large corporations, often monopolies in their fields. The
workers are unionized, have job security, earn high wages, and are
usually white. The secondary sector is comprised of those working
in smaller companies in very competitive industries. The workers are

not likely to be unionized, they are paid poorly and have no job security. It is generally understood that minorities tend to work in this sector. Their jobs are unstable, particularly vulnerable to the ups and downs in the economy, and the workers suffer a high rate of unemployment. New immigrants, who do not speak English, are at a particular disadvantage. They fall to the bottom of this secondary sector, the last to be hired and the first to be fired.

Chinatown workers, according to this labor pattern, should belong to the secondary sector. Yet immigrants working for Chinese employers are not competing for jobs in the larger labor market. While they receive low wages and experience high job turnover rates, they have no problem finding jobs in Chinatown. Further, their employability and income in the Chinatown economy are not markedly improved by knowledge of English or length of residence in this country. It follows, then, that the Chinese immigrants can survive without learning English or having to integrate into the larger labor market. Some social scientists are so impressed with the Chinatown economy that they suggest it might pose a new alternative for immigrant mobility. According to this view, the Chinese are taking care of themselves; Chinese workers willingly work for Chinese employers, to create a dynamic economy in which success is shared by all. Some even go so far as to suggest the existence of a deal between the workers and employers based on ethnic solidarity and mutual benefit.

The alliance between Chinese owners and their workers is unfortunately a myth. The "blessings" simply disguise the misery of the workers. The majority of new immigrants confront a double trap: the racially segmented American labor market and the harsh labor conditions of the Chinatown economy.

EXPLOITATION OF THE CHINESE WORKERS

Those who work for Chinese bosses soon learn that all standard American labor practices are ignored. The central premise for economic development in Chinatown is cheap labor. Waiters and shop clerks are expected to work six days a week, more than ten hours a day, with no compensation for overtime, no holidays, and no sick leaves. They are paid below the minimum wage: a shop clerk gets $600 a month for a 60-hour week, and most waiters are paid $200 a month, earning the rest of their income from tips. In large and busy restaurants, waiters don't even receive wages; their income consists entirely of tips. Most waiters have to chip in two-thirtieths of their tips to management, to divide among the other personnel. In 1980 a dispute on this very issue triggered a major strike at the Silver Palace, the largest restaurant in Chinatown, when the management wanted waiters to share more of their tips with others.

The owners see themselves as victims of competition from American businesses as well as from fellow Chinese. From their point of view, they are fighting for survival; therefore, they have to cut costs to the minimum. Employees get no health and accident insurance. When a worker is sick or cannot come to work for any reason, he must find and pay a substitute. Moreover, restaurant owners are not concerned with maintaining a healthy and safe working environment; the cost is too expensive. Air and grease filters in kitchens are rarely in working order; thus harmful pollutants are spread to the work force and into the street. Bathrooms in most restaurants are never tidy; they usually do not have toilet tissue, soap, hot water, or towels. Emergency fire exits are regularly blocked to keep thieves from breaking in. Finally, most restaurant owners do not train new workers; they are expected to learn from the complaints of impatient patrons, the scoldings of chefs and bosses, and the insults of disgruntled fellow waiters.

Such harsh labor practices are so firmly entrenched that even the garment workers in the community, who are all members of the International Ladies Garment Workers Union, face similar outrageous conditions. The employers continue to ignore regulations regarding the forty-hour workweek and health and safety provisions. According to the 1982 ILGWU contract, the minimum piece rate should be $5.25 an hour. Yet workers will tell you that contractors change piece rates daily, to the point that the average worker cannot keep up with shifting calculations and rarely receives even the national minimum wage, let alone the union minimum.

This is ironic. Chinese were once barred from membership in American unions. Now they hold unionized garment-factory jobs. However, the sites of their jobs are in Chinatown, and their union has not helped them to enjoy the full benefits and protection that other American workers have.

The Chinese are driven by a grueling incentive system. Waiters work hard to get more tips; garment workers work faster to complete more pieces. It is said that Chinese employees work like slaves, but the workers become their own slave drivers. These are jobs for the young, who have the energy to work furiously in order to earn more money. In fact, a few particularly hardworking waiters in a large, busy restaurant can make up to $1,500 a month, tax free. However, after a few years, most workers suffer job-induced ailments: foot problems for the waiters, backache and blurred vision for the garment workers. A seamstress must then request less strenuous tasks, such as cutting threads or folding garments, at even lower wages. A waiter will have to search for work in a less popular or a suburban restaurant, where the pace is not so fast—but at much less income. The prospect for an immigrant who remains in Chinatown as a worker is downward mobility.

Under these circumstances, why don't immigrants leave the trap? Theoretically, immigrants who decide at the outset not to work in Chinatown will, in the long run, attain greater upward mobility. But immigrants do not really have a choice. Because they have language problems and a lack of job skills, those leaving Chinatown will end up working in the highly competitive secondary labor market, competing with other racial minorities for low-paying jobs with frequent layoffs and unemployment.

STABLE AND
PRODUCTIVE WORKERS

Chinese employers maintain a virtual monopoly over the Chinatown work force. They can get away with abuses of all kinds.

It is common for an arriving garment worker to be told to go home for lack of work. The layoff may last a week—or a few months. On the other hand, when the factory is busy, workers are expected to work overtime without extra pay. In a Chinese restaurant, the workers may be told at the end of a shift that the restaurant will be going out of business on the following day and that their services will no longer be needed.

Normally, workers in the secondary market, confronted by very low wages, wretched working conditions, and irregular employment, become discouraged. They drop out of the labor market and subsist on unemployment insurance and welfare. Chinatown workers, on the other hand, will not apply for handouts, because this would be an admission of defeat in their dream of a better life. They look for new jobs immediately, to remain in the Chinatown work force.

Despite indefinite layoffs, garment workers will go right back to work as soon as a contractor calls. They are housewives with children, with limited job skills and language problems; they are told constantly by the employers that they are lucky to have jobs. Although the contractors pay them below the minimum wage, and lay them off regularly, they still come back. Most importantly, the owners share an information network and control the work force with a black list that helps them to weed out undisciplined or activist workers.

CHINESE ETHNIC MOBILITY

The American economy and the Chinatown social structure limit the options for Chinatown workers. Unlike other immigrants to America, the Chinese cannot follow the traditional path of mobility. In the past, European immigrants came as unskilled laborers. Once they learned English, they moved into higher-paying, semi-skilled jobs in the larger labor market. Slowly they joined unions, acquired skills, and earned higher wages. Eventually they, or their children, moved out of the working class altogether by starting small businesses or pursuing professional careers. However, the critical first step for the immigrant was to become part of the American labor force. Today, the racial segmentation of the U.S. labor market effectively excludes the Chinese immigrants from taking this path.

Faced with the uncertainties of the secondary labor sector, the Chinese immigrant is tempted to stay in Chinatown. There are readily available jobs and an ethnically familiar environment. However, Chinatown is like a warm bath—once a new immigrant decides to settle in, it is difficult to get out, even as the water slowly becomes cold. However, once inside Chinatown, the immigrants find that mobility is limited. There is only one path upward: to become the owner of a business.

Most Chinese workers want to own their own enterprise, or to enter into partnership with friends or relatives. This is the traditional path of success for overseas Chinese. In Southeast Asia, for instance, where the Chinese migrated years ago, they worked hard at manual labor and saved all they could to start small retail or service businesses. The survival of their businesses depended on strong family and kin-ship ties. For example, one Chinese might start out by hiring relatives and fellow villagers. Once his business prospered, he would assist those who helped him to start their own businesses. Later they, too, would branch out. That's why one often finds Chinese businessmen dominating one particular trade in a country, with many of the owners related.

Chinatown residents still believe in this path to success, despite different conditions in the United States. For one thing, the scale of economic development is much larger and not limited to small retail and service trades. When you have an employer hiring hundreds of people not related to him, kinship and clan relationships increasingly give way to association along class lines. The old collective business arrangement still exists but is not a vital factor in the economy. The chances for success are also slimmer.

Entering the garment-manufacturing and restaurant businesses is costly and uncertain, particularly in recent times of rising real-estate speculation and high interest rates. To open a first-class restaurant, the owner must spend at least $500,000 for renovation alone. A small garment factory may be cheaper, but small factories must compete against dozens of large operations, each hiring up to 200 workers; a number of owners own more than five factories. A large outfit, like Lam's Fashion Group, comprised of fifteen factories, employs 1,200 workers. It has standing contracts with profitable manufacturers like Evan Picone, Liz Claiborne, and Leslie Fay, and does up to $40 million of business a year.[6] It is not easy for a small beginner to compete against such an entrepreneur.

Business failures are high; few new restaurants in Chinatown last more than a year. Of the 500 garment factories in operation in 1985, 40 percent did not exist two years earlier.[7] In other words, the start-up rate of Chinese businesses is high, but the failure rate is high as well. Almost all the restaurant workers I have interviewed had tried, at one time or another, to open their own restaurants, and failed.

In the 1980s, business in Chinatown reached the point of saturation: too many immigrants, too many new businesses, and exorbitant rents. Suicidal competition developed throughout the community. A price war between Chinese travel agencies depressed the round-trip airfare to Hong Kong to as little as $600 (the usual price is close to $1,000). Restaurants, hoping to lure nearby office workers, offered lunch specials—including soup, meat, and vegetables, a glass of wine and dessert—for $4.95. Nearby competition immediately lowered the price to $3.95. Prices on the menus have not increased in recent years, even at the fancy new restaurants. Chinese food in Chinatown is a bargain!

Competition of this kind is damaging in more ways than one. It leads to even lower wages and longer hours for the workers. Simultaneously, corners are cut: more monosodium glutamate is used in cooking to artificially enhance flavors; cleaning and sanitation costs are cut. Every week several Chinese restaurants are cited by the city's Department of Health for violating sanitary standards. The result is a downward spiral: fewer returning customers, more cost-cutting, lower wages, crankier waiters, unmotivated chefs, further loss of customers.

OTHER OPTIONS

The depressed situation in Chinatown is increasingly forcing people to seek survival outside the community. But moving into the American labor market is difficult. Most high-paying jobs require a minimum proficiency in English and satisfactory scores on written exams. One waiter, after working in Chinese restaurants for twenty-five years, decided to become a subway booth attendant; but he could not pass the required examination because of his poor English and lack of self-confidence. Younger immigrants with an American high-school education are far more likely to get these jobs.

Several social agencies, especially the Chinatown Manpower Project, receive federal funding to provide training programs for new immigrants. Participants are paid to learn special skills and, at the same time, to learn English. Still, this training may not help people in their late thirties or those who have worked many years in Chinatown. Furthermore, with recent drastic cuts in these programs, the agencies tend to select younger persons, who are more likely to succeed.

The prospects for middle-aged Chinatown workers are not good. They need to earn and save enough before it's too late. Thus, it is no accident that gambling is so popular. On one hand, the Chinese fondness for gambling is historic. Marco Polo more than six centuries ago commented in his diary on the amazing popularity of gambling in China. Chinatown workers gamble, and gamble big, in an infinite number of ways and places: at OTB (Off-Track Betting) parlors; with numbers; on lottery tickets; in Chinatown basement gambling halls or Atlantic City casinos. The two local OTB offices boast the largest volume of business in the city. There are even two Chinese-language racing sheets for bettors. For the incurable addicts, a coffee shop on Pell Street, where racing enthusiasts exchange tips, is open twenty-four hours a day.

This fondness for gambling can be understood as a way to release tension from long hours of boring labor, as an acceptable form of social interaction, and, most of all, as a means of escape. Waiters gamble during their off-hours between the lunch and dinner rush, often with the restaurant owner joining them. It is easy to lose $50 in less than ten minutes. They get credit from friends, or even from their bosses. To pay back losses, they work longer hours, which increases their tension and intensifies their desire to win big. They face an increasingly desperate situation. Community service centers regularly report that many Chinatown families are torn apart because of this addiction.

"MY KIDS ARE MAKING IT!"

Most immigrants come to the United States because they see no future in their home country. Chinese from the Far East have additional worries over political uncertainties. Many, particularly the young, want a new beginning. Others pin their hopes on their children. Some, despite expecting limited achievements for themselves, seek opportunities for their offspring. If the next generation can succeed by joining the American middle class and moving out of the ghetto, parents see their American dream fulfilled and all their hard work and self-sacrifice worthwhile.

In the last several decades second-generation Chinese Americans have shown a high degree of upward mobility. A significant number have entered professional and white-collar jobs. Only a few continue in the trades of their immigrant parents. There are less than a handful of American-born Chinese working in the garment factories. Simi-

larly, there are very few in the restaurant business, except in management positions.

The second generation's economic gains make geographic mobility
possible. Few American-born Chinese continue to live in New York's
Chinatown, except for the relatively few in the new middle class
housing developments, like Confucius Plaza or Chatham Towers.
Most prefer the suburbs. The second generation began to move out
of Chinatown in the 1950s, when there was still discrimination in
many neighborhoods. Enclaves of middle-class Chinese developed,
often with a small community center. In Hempstead, Long Island,
for instance, there is a community center with a Chinese-language
school, a women's committee, and other social supports. Today,
middle-class Chinese live in a wide variety of suburban neighborhoods.

CONFUCIAN TRADITION
OF LEARNING?

Younger generations of Chinese are achieving upward mobility through education. They have earned respect for their intellectual accomplishments, particularly in the difficult subjects of science and technology. There is truth to the belief that Chinese families
stress education—and that Chinese students have most certainly worked
hard to achieve fine academic records.

The influence that explains the high academic achievement is the
family and community environment. Immigrant parents tend to transfer
their intense ambitions to their children. These are further reinforced
in the community. Good grades in school and entering a first-rate
college are praised not only by the family but by relatives and family
friends. There's constant pressure and supervision of the young to
develop discipline and, most importantly, to internalize their parents'
values as their own. As a result, many youths grow up with a high
regard for hard work and accomplishment. The Chinese immigrants
are not unique in this way. Earlier immigrants, such as the Jews,

and more recent groups, such as the Koreans, also value education
highly.

Unfortunately, there is a tendency to generalize that all Chinese
are good students. Historically, this has not been true. Emphasis on
education came only with the opening of job opportunities after
World War II. Until then, Chinese youth were depicted as either
hatchet men or "singsong girls," from Chinatowns known for tong
wars and opium dens. Barred from jobs outside Chinatown, the
youth were forced to work in low-paying service jobs. Very few
American-born Chinese pursued a college education.[8] The few that
did studied medicine and dentistry, and opened offices in Chinatown.
Those with other professional degrees could not find work; some
even had to go to China for jobs. During World War II, with the
easing of racial barriers in employment, job opportunities began to
change for youth. The Chinese then pursued college educations in
order to enter these new white-collar occupations.

The Chinese achievement in education is sometimes attributed to
a traditional reverence for learning. Indeed, many Chinese perpetuate
this myth, claiming that the Chinese respect knowledge because of
their Confucian cultural background. A simpler explanation is that
the Chinese pursue higher education for very practical reasons. However, there is no truth to the belief that the Chinese have a greater
respect for knowledge than other groups. If that were the case, the
Chinese selection of college majors would spread across many academic disciplines. As it is, few Chinese go into humanities and social
sciences; most concentrate on technical fields and engineering science. Even when it comes to science, the Chinese study applied
sciences—fields in which they are most likely to get jobs—like medicine, engineering, and computer science. Even those who major in
business tend to concentrate on the more technical aspects, such as
accounting and corporate taxation. Until recently, few went into
law. Older immigrants tend to see careers in law as too political,
associating politics with the period of civil wars in China.

The claim linking Chinese achievement in education to Confu-
cianism is a myth. Confucius's greatest legacy was the structuring of

a political and social order in ancient China. Scholars were the highest class, ranking above farmers, menial laborers, and merchants. An elaborate examination system selected learned individuals for government positions. Imperial exams demanded mastery of the classics, calligraphy, and formal essay writing. Over time, the requirements became increasingly rigid and dependent on memorization and creative thinking was stifled. Nevertheless, passing the examinations opened the way to upward mobility. The young were told to study hard, pass the exams, and become government officials; fame, status, and prosperity would automatically follow. Learning, thus, had a very practical objective: education was a means of breaking through the class barriers of ancient Chinese society.

Furthermore, individuals steeped in this Confucian tradition were not prepared to deal with the requirements of modern learning. In fact, every reform movement in China since the last century has considered the Confucian education system an obstacle to the creative thinking needed for modernization.

Other myths about Chinese academic accomplishments persist. Aside from the assumption that all Chinese are good at studies, it is also believed that rising education levels have automatically brought upward mobility. However, the evidence seems to suggest that not all Chinese have an equal opportunity. There is a large difference in educational opportunities between the children of Uptown and Downtown Chinese. The Uptown youth clearly have a superior academic environment. Most winners of the national scholastic awards are the offspring of professionals from Taiwan or of stranded scholars. In the last few years almost one-quarter of the top winners of the Westinghouse Science Talent Search, the nation's most prestigious award for American high-school students, went to youth of Chinese descent. In 1987, there were nine Chinese out of the forty finalists. Of the nine, five either were born in or had parents from Taiwan; and six had parents who were research scientists, physicians, or college professors.[9]

Furthermore, the majors chosen by the Uptown and Downtown groups are somewhat different, as shown by a survey of the Chinese students at the City University of New York. In 1985, close to 5,000 Chinese were attending the city system, with a majority enrolled in science and technical fields. However, a disproportionate number of the students from Chinatown were attending Baruch College of the city university system, majoring in accounting and business.

The Chinese students in Ivy League colleges are mostly the off-spring of the Uptown Chinese. Ironically, very few Downtown Chinese profit from the affirmative-action programs at those schools. Today some institutions are restricting Chinese admissions because of over-representation. This racial backlash severely affects the Downtown Chinese, who need affirmative action that the Uptown Chinese don't need.

PRESENT REALITIES

The sad reality is that even as many laud the achievements of Chinese students, Chinatown schools have fallen on hard times. The situation has worsened since 1979, with the influx of immigrants from the People's Republic of China. Much of the schools' work now is to provide remedial instruction. A 1984 Board of Education report showed that all the schools in Chinatown were rated far below citywide standards. Among the four local elementary schools, only 28.4 percent of the students reached the standard English reading level; the citywide average was 55 percent.[10] At Seward Park High School on the Lower East Side 97 percent of the Chinese students were above the normal age for their grade levels. More than thirty students were over twenty-one; they were still studying for their high-school diplomas.[11] Other Chinatown schools are also over-whelmed. Of the 600 students in P.S. 1 (an elementary school), there are 200 immigrants. According to the principal, there is insufficient funding to provide the bilingual instruction they need.[12]

The problems are severe at the three public high schools (Seward Park, Washington Irving, and Lower East Side Prep) with very high percentages of students from Chinatown. In 1985 they were among the seventy-two schools singled out as the worst of the six hundred schools in the city.[13] Not only did students at these schools have poor reading and writing skills, they also had exceedingly high drop-out and truancy rates.

Newly arrived immigrant youngsters are more likely to have problems in school; when the volume of immigration is high, the schools lack resources to keep up with it. Chinatown schools in the 1960s and 1970s experienced this problem. However, the students then were mainly from Hong Kong and Taiwan, where the education standards were relatively high and education is free to all children up to the ninth grade. Students must pass examinations in order to be promoted to the next grade. If they fail, they have to repeat the grade. The children were accustomed to rigorous schoolwork. When they came to this country, the workload seemed very light. It did not take them too much time to catch up, despite the language deficiency. Also, Taiwan and Hong Kong have both experienced American culture through movies, TV, and advertising, easing their transition into the new environment.

However, since 1979, large numbers of students have been coming from the People's Republic of China, often from rural villages in Kwangtung province. The education system there is quite poor, and the students are totally unprepared for American education. Few know English at all; most have to start from the beginning. Judging from Board of Education reports, their entrance into Chinatown schools has brought about falling proficiency scores. The prospect is for further decline, as more immigrants arrive and the schools fail to commit sufficient resources to meet their needs.

Still, English proficiency is only part of the problem. The high attrition and high truancy rates are much more serious, reflecting larger social and economic issues. Chinatown, for reasons already discussed, has faced growing economic problems in the 1980s. Residents are working more and making less. Most students have to work after school to supplement family income; social workers report that many students work more than thirty hours a week. More than half claim that their families are dependent on their earnings. These

youth have little time and energy to study, and little opportunity to
practice English. Their parents also work long hours and hardly see
their children, let alone supervise them. Many parents know little
about this country; some do not know enough English to read their
children's report cards. Yet they demand obedience and good per-
formance in school. Huge emotional gaps develop between the generations. Family counselors are regularly asked by frustrated parents
to intervene in serious disputes they have with their children: Parents
complain of their insubordination and laziness in school; the children, in turn, accuse their parents of authoritarian behavior. Therefore, the high dropout rate is the result of a combination of factors:
discouragement because of language problems, a heavy outside workload, family problems, and lack of financial support.

Conditions in the bustling environment in Chinatown are not
conducive to youth development. There are very few gyms available,
few places for young people to socialize, and few places to go for
advice. The school system is overcrowded; furthermore, there are
too few bilingual teachers and counselors in Chinatown. The existing
social-service and church after-school programs are useful, but they
lack qualified youth workers.

These conditions provide fertile soil for youth gangs. Gang members, recruited by adults, are paid to guard gambling houses, to carry
out extortion threats, to intimidate local residents, and to serve as
runners in the drug traffic. Gang violence is tied into real-estate
speculation and business competition. Killings happen regularly, and
many crimes are not even reported to the local police precinct. How
does this square with the myth that Chinese youngsters are orderly
and there are very few delinquents?

There is a crisis for the youth in Chinatown. And it will not go
away. To ignore reality is irresponsible. Many studies indicate that
those who have direct contact with youth understand the gravity of
the situation, but our willingness to accept myths makes the job of
helping them all the more difficult.

UNEXPECTED
IMMIGRANTS

One often hears: "The Chinese are not doing that badly—after all, the second generation always makes it." Counting on the next generation is not a sure bet these days. In addition, it is disturbing that so many accept the suffering of the first generation as natural and necessary. "What decent conditions should you expect from people who don't speak English and have no skills?" "The immigrants don't mind—even these conditions are better than what they had at home." Some people go on to suggest that their own immigrant ancestors experienced the same hardships: they worked in sweatshops but never complained. And their offspring made it.

These arguments miss the point. First, the offspring of immigrants who are treated as second-class citizens will not be treated as equals by other Americans. Second, the history of the American labor movement shows that new immigrants have played a vital role in improving working conditions for all in their adopted country. Third, the treatment of earlier immigrants was wrong then and it is wrong now. It cannot be rationalized, especially not in the 1980s, after the impressive gains in labor organizing and civil rights over the past fifty years.

A new generation of immigrants, including the Chinese, has come to the United States at a time when the American work force is being restructured. One of the cornerstones of the 1965 Immigration Act was to shift admission priorities from unskilled laborers to skilled professionals, since America was moving toward a post-industrial economy.

In the last twenty years, the United States has witnessed a steady decline of industrial jobs, because multinational corporations have switched production to overseas. As these jobs are moved to Third World countries—such as Taiwan, Korea, and Brazil—American industrial workers suffer high rates of unemployment. And yet at this time, large numbers of unskilled immigrants have entered through the "Uniting the Family" provisions or as illegal immigrants. Not only are they here—many are employed in manufacturing jobs. Garment sweatshops have mushroomed in Chinatown and uptown Manhattan.

This phenomenon—the decline of the traditional industrial work force and the rise of new industries based on immigrant labor—seems contradictory. Some explain it by suggesting that the American economy has undergone not only restructuring at the base—from manufacturing to high-tech and service industries—but also restructuring of the labor force. This occurred as the relative power between workers and management has been reshaped, through substitution of low-wage, unorganized workers for high-wage, organized labor.[14] Immigrants play a key role in this pattern. This accounts for the continued and rapid flow of immigrants from Asia, the Caribbean, and Latin America at a time when many American workers are unemployed. The large influx of unskilled Chinese immigrants can be explained by this same logic. Ironically, as in the past, today's economic developments have placed Chinese immigrants at the center of conflict between capital and labor.

When Chinese immigrants first came to this country in the nineteenth century, they were used as strikebreakers. The new wave of unskilled Chinese immigrants has come as U.S. organized labor is in decline: industrial jobs have decreased, union membership has fallen, competition from imports has increased; the union rank and file has become disenchanted with its leadership; and government policy has become hostile to organized labor. The Chinese are not fighting for jobs in the American labor market as they were one hundred years ago. They are working in Chinatown for Chinese employers. But their productivity, as well as that of other immigrants, is often used by employers in the larger society to justify lower wages and fewer benefits for other American workers.

In order to fully comprehend the implications of this argument, we need to understand what productivity really means. Productivity is measured by dividing the output of labor by the input management provides in production (all calculated in dollar values). The lower the wages, the lower the input, and therefore the higher the productivity. But lowering wages is not the only way to increase productivity. Reduction of other production costs also reduces employers' input. Thus, cuts in social security and retirement benefits; the elimination of sick pay, vacation and overtime pay; and cuts in expenditure for safety and health care all increase productivity. Finally, employers can add to productivity by increasing the output of workers. This can be achieved through mechanization or through tightening workplace discipline.

In American society there are laws that protect workers by limiting how far the employers may go in increasing productivity. Many Chinatown workers, however, are working in an underground economy, where American labor laws do not apply.

UNDERGROUND
ECONOMY

Generally, the "underground economy" is comprised of activities beyond the control of government authorities. In the past the term was mostly used to describe the activities of organized crime. Today the underground economy encompasses a much larger segment of society, although media attention seems to focus on the question of tax evasion. Thus, some economists see the growth of the underground economy as a revolt by small businesses which have been taxed to the point of stagnation.

Anyone familiar with Chinatown realizes that an underground economy has long existed there. Restaurants, garment factories, and other businesses operate regularly with two sets of books in order to underreport income and evade taxes; the workers and suppliers are paid off the books. Workers are not expected to report their full income either, so they supposedly benefit also. However, underground economic practices in Chinatown are not limited to tax matters. Local businesses regularly violate commercial rules. Employers routinely ignore fair labor practices.

The underground economy in Chinatown has many defenders.

Conservative economists feel that its development is a natural re-action to an overcontrolled and overregulated economy. They believe it will force government to eliminate outdated laws and to get off the back of business. High productivity, they believe, can be achieved through unfettered free enterprise with minimal government inter-vention. What these economists completely disregard is the impact on workers in the underground economy. Invariably there is a re-surgence of labor practices that belong to an earlier period of cap-italism: seventy-hour workweeks, near-starvation wages, and ruthless supervision.

These are the current working conditions in much of Chinatown, and they are worsening. Sweatshops are now commonplace; increas-ingly, one also encounters home work and child labor.

Yet some still insist that Chinatown is a model of productivity. There are even suggestions for legislation which would legalize the underground economy as "free-enterprise zones" in ghetto areas such as the South Bronx and Harlem. To encourage investment, busi-nesses would receive tax breaks and relaxed labor regulations. Such free-enterprise zones already exist in many Third World countries, where their governments have in effect surrendered sovereignty over certain regions to multinational corporations.

The Chinatown underground economy is this country's free-enterprise zone, except that it's not legal. It is maintained by the informal political structure in Chinatown, with the tacit agreement of outside government officials.

CHINATOWN'S INFORMAL POLITICAL STRUCTURE

5

CHINATOWN'S employers can exploit working people because they are able to ignore minimum labor standards without worrying about government enforcement. Historically, government officials have not intervened in Chinatown unless there was uncontrolled gang violence, large-scale drug trafficking, smuggling of illegal aliens, or other crimes that might affect the peace and security of the society at large. However, this policy of non-intervention is not *neutral*. Lack of government intervention has meant *de facto* rule of the community by a traditional Chinatown elite. This elite operates outside the American political system; it is an informal political structure.

The internal workings of isolated ethnic communities are rarely studied, because of our social scientists' prevailing concern with the integration of immigrants into American society. The institutions and organizational structures within an immigrant community are seen as cultural baggage to be left behind, something not worth detailed analysis. The institutions that are studied tend to be sensational ones, such as the Italian Mafia. Even then, the Mafia is regarded as a criminal organization, and rarely analyzed in the context of the evolution of the Italian community or its relationship to the broader American political structure. Similarly, everyone reads about tong wars and Chinese gang killings, but most people do not see these activities as related to the overall social and political structure of Chinatown.

The underground economy in Chinatown revolves around the community's informal political structure, which maintains and regulates the economy, allowing employers to both underpay and overwork the immigrants. Thus, the community structure creates the so-called competitive edge of Chinatown workers.

This political structure existed in New York's Chinatown as early as the 1880s. Since the community remained in relative isolation until the 1960s, the structure had a long time to evolve and has, as a result, solidified. Having acquired a momentum of its own, it is still operative, despite profound external changes in recent years.

The institutional structure was originally brought here by immigrants from rural regions in China during the Ch'ing Dynasty. However, under American conditions, it has been dramatically transformed. To understand the present political structure, we need to consider its origin.

INFORMAL POLITICAL STRUCTURE IN IMPERIAL CHINA

When Chinese laborers first arrived in California in the 1840s, American authorities gave them no protection. The newcomers had few legal rights. Governmental neglect was not new to these immigrants, since the Chinese imperial system, while highly centralized (above the county and district levels), provided very limited control in their home rural villages. Therefore, even before arriving in American Chinatowns, the immigrants were familiar with the functioning of an informal political structure in their society.

The Chinese imperial government was primarily interested in collecting taxes and preventing local rebellions. District magistrates, the "mother and father officials," as they were familiarly called, were the lowest echelon of imperial representatives. Theoretically, they attended to local political needs. Presumably they collected taxes, arbitrated family and property disputes, ensured local peace, tried and convicted criminals, handled local grievances, and supervised the district examinations. But due to the size of the local populations, the magistrates could not carry out all their duties. The imperial government, for its part, wanted to make sure that its local representatives did not develop too close a relationship with the people under their jurisdiction. District magistrates were assigned a maximum of three years in any locality; as a result, they never stayed long enough to become familiar with local issues. Most were simply interested in a tenure without problems; they avoided controversial issues, particularly if they involved powerful local interests. The magistrates preferred to have problems resolved by existing traditional arrangements.[1]

The central government in Peking, therefore, accepted a degree of local autonomy. And so an informal political structure developed around clans, trade guilds, secret societies, and a variety of benevolent local associations.[2] In the absence of an active official government, people were forced to rely on an informal structure for protection and for the adjudication of disputes involving business transactions and other matters.

In rural villages, the basic political units were the clans—large, extended families comprising several generations—sometimes encompassing the whole village. Normal family and property disputes could be resolved within the clan. Some clans were large enough to sponsor schools and courts, and to provide health services and general welfare programs. When disputes developed between individuals belonging to different clans, the member of the more powerful clan had the advantage since a clan's power was based on the size of its landholdings and wealth, as well as the ability of its members to pass official examinations to attain the status of scholars. The latter had special privileges, including access to the district magistrate's office. Power was derived from access.

The structure of a clan was hierarchical. Its leaders provided protection and representation for all members. Connection with a powerful leader could improve a member's status and economic position. Thus, the more powerful a leader, the more willing people were to join the clan, further extending its power. A strong clan was able to expand its interests at the expense of other groups, even to the point of undermining the power of the imperial government. Smaller clans had to form alliances with one another, or establish alternative groups, such as trade guilds and secret societies, to counter the power of the larger clans.

Thus clans, guilds, associations, and secret societies played the central role in local politics. Protection, status, and opportunities all came from belonging to a united, well-organized group. The rules within these groups were based not on legal or ethical concerns but rather on the loyalty and cohesion of their members.

In times of political crisis, the imperial government needed the support of local elites to maintain its control, and loyal groups would be given more autonomy and legitimacy. Eventually local groups formed their own armies, since the garrison troops of the imperial government were not concerned with banditry and minor intervillage warfare.[3]

Once local clans had their own forces, they could use them in interclan warfare to enhance their landholdings and power. Such initiatives brought about a proliferation of private armies. In times of famine and political instability, these local forces could initiate revolt against the imperial government.[4] A state of anarchy developed and was soon out of control. Several major peasant rebellions during the nineteenth century started at the village level. The largest, the Taiping Rebellion (1850–64), almost succeeded in overthrowing the Ch'ing Dynasty by occupying the southern half of the country. The leader of the rebellion, Hung Hsiu-ch'uan, came from Hua-hsien, near Canton, in the area where the majority of early Chinese

Americans originally came from. His rise to power was initially helped by regional secret societies and clans.

People from Kwangtung have the strongest clan and lineage ties among all Chinese. They maintained these ties when they moved to northern urban centers and even when they emigrated abroad. Without a modern concept of nationalism, their consciousness was based on clan and regional ties. This consciousness was heightened by the imperial government's neglect of the Kwangtung region, which was regarded as a marginal area of the empire. The central government provided Kwangtung with few services and little protection. As a result, an informal political structure developed and grew strong.

THUS, WHEN Cantonese immigrants found their relationship to the U.S. authorities similar to what it had been under the Ch'ing government, they transplanted the traditional political institutions to Chinatown.

The early immigrants to America, as mentioned before, came mainly from a small area in Kwangtung and tended to establish a new home where other clan and village folk had already settled. This pattern caused immigrants from the same clans, villages, and districts to concentrate in particular American cities. In old New York Chinatown (before the 1950s), more than 50 percent of the people came from Toishan; a large number were named Tam, Wong, or Lee. As a result, family, clan, village, guild, and other groups were easily re-established. The Chinese considered these mutual-aid groups and claimed that people joined them voluntarily. Furthermore, these community organizations were described as cultural and nonpolitical in nature. Their initial conception may have been nonpolitical, but inevitably the groups became very political indeed.

FONGS

Relatives, family friends, and fellow villagers of early immigrants relied on one another when they first arrived. Mostly bachelors, they customarily shared an apartment in order to save money.

It was common in an expensive city like New York to have a dozen people living in a single apartment. Even today, many apartments in Chinatown have wall-to-wall beds, each one occupied by three Chinese in successive eight-hour shifts. As more people came, the group would branch out, and the original apartment turned into a club room. Through games of mah-jongg or poker the immigrants made contacts to obtain jobs, found partners for joint ventures, and discussed the pooling or borrowing of funds for new businesses. The club room was also used to provide temporary accommodations for the newly arrived and the unemployed. The people in such a circle evolved into a collective called a *fong*, literally, a "room." Members of a fong, often as many as fifty to one hundred, were from the same village, had the same surname, or worked in the same trade: they developed a close contact and great loyalty to one another.

VILLAGE, SURNAME, DISTRICT, AND SPEECH-PATTERN ASSOCIATIONS

Several fongs from the same village formed a village association; fongs of the same surname formed family or surname associations. These associations carried out functions to support one another; they could accomplish more through collective action, particularly when dealing with common concerns over the situation at home in China. A village association would raise funds for famine relief or for the building of schools and hospitals in the home village. In the 1920s, during the warlord period, various associations sent money home, so that relatives could buy arms and build fortifications for protection against bandits. In fact, in Kwangtung there still remain many of these well-built, castle-like, granite fortifications, some rising as high as five stories above the rural landscape.

Some immigrants came from villages or clans with small memberships and limited power. To create larger groupings, immigrants from contiguous villages who spoke similar subdialects of Cantonese joined to form a *huiguan*. While huiguans continued to carry out mutual-aid and charity functions—such as maintaining a cemetery or providing medicine and burial expenses for the poor—they were much more commercially oriented. Huiguans arbitrated disputes among members and served as credit and employment agencies. In business transactions with others, they ensured their members' obligations. Thus, a huiguan often acted as a general collection agency and creditor for its more affluent members.[5] Before the 1950s, any Chinese intending to depart for China had to report to his huiguan to make sure that he had paid all his debts and fulfilled his financial obligations.

The many associations existing in Chinatown were essential for survival; they formed a collective defense against the hostile larger society. They also provided order within the community. To this extent, the associations were functional; the members did join voluntarily. However, once established, the associations generated a momentum of their own. They began to operate with a set of rules and a system of logic independent of the wishes of the membership.

Relationships within an association were not exactly mutual or equal. Members who owned shops and restaurants commanded respect because other members depended on them for jobs. Those who received favors became followers, forming patron/client relationships. Clients depended on the patron for help in securing jobs, mediating personal conflicts, and providing protection. Patrons, being owners of businesses, became leaders in the association. They were the "big shots," or *kiu ling* in Cantonese (*chiao-lin*, according to the Mandarin pronunciation), meaning a leader in an overseas community.

Kiu lings were the active and generous members of their associations, because they pledged the most money during fund-raising drives. Their names and the amount of their contributions were published in local newspapers and displayed prominently on red strips of paper hanging on the walls of the association headquarters. They became elected officers or members of the executive board.

The elected leaders enjoyed great prestige, which they used in the business community to form profitable partnerships. Since the associations operated with few established rules and did not follow American legal practices, they were not held to account for money collected from the membership. If the elected officers were from powerful clans and were not men of integrity, they could purchase or sell property for the association and pocket the profits.[6]

These kui lings had property, official position, and the backing of their associations. A hierarchy based on wealth developed within the associations. Above all, the associations were the means by which Chinatown's merchant class maintained social control.

THE DEFENSIVE AND OFFENSIVE NATURE OF THE ASSOCIATIONS

As a collective, an association acted to defend its members. Whenever a member became involved with institutions of the larger society, the association's English-speaking secretary acted as his interpreter, defender, and negotiator. The association also developed an "offensive" capacity and helped members develop their personal business interests; this on occasion led to the establishment of a monopoly in one trade, created by pooling members' resources to set up operations that would undersell the competition and force it out of business. Or direct means were used—such as violence. Some large associations to this day retain gang members for just that purpose.

Most commonly, associations set up spheres of influence in sections of Chinatown. Once territories were established, only their members could operate businesses within that area. Because Chinatown is small and the fighting intense, most conflicts developed around competition for territory.

Ownership of buildings was the ultimate sign of power. Every association had to have its headquarters located in the territory it claimed. Members would contribute toward the purchase of a building. Eventually they would try to buy adjacent buildings. Businesses within the territory were operated only by members of the association, or by individuals who were willing to accept its dominance. For decades most of the buildings and shops on the upper end of Mott Street have been owned by the Lees. They are the most powerful family association in Chinatown, and own a tall new headquarters building with a marble façade.

In old Chinatown, one's economic position, i.e., one's ability to get a good job or operate a prosperous business, was determined by membership in an association. The larger and more powerful the association, the greater the advantages for the individual. Businessmen needed an association, lest they be squeezed out by someone with more powerful backing. So, in order to survive, people joined associations. Membership was not voluntary.

Since everyone wanted to belong to a powerful association, associations which were weak had to form alliances with one another. For instance, the Lun Kan Association was formed by people with four different surnames: Chang, Kwan, Liu, and Chow. This union claimed its origin from the four heroes in the famous historical novel *The Three Kingdoms*, set in the second and third century A.D. Others without readily available historical claims would form tongs or Triads based on secret brotherhood principles. Or they established associations around trades, such as the Chinese Hand Laundry Alliance or the Lian Yee Seamen's Association.

The rules of the game in Chinatown made associations and organizations the basic legitimate entities. Unaffiliated individuals, even with fame and money, were not recognized. New groups are constantly emerging: the Chinese Consolidated Democratic Club, the Progressive Chinese Association, the Acupuncturists' Association, among others. There are at present some three hundred different associations in Chinatown.

Individuals joined associations for protection, and for the maintenance—and expansion—of their interests. By its nature, an association was exclusionary. Inevitably this led to conflicts with other

associations. In times of conflict, members rallied around their own
associations, creating more sectarian differences. That's why Chinatown has always been an extremely divided community—though the
impression of outsiders is different.

THE GOVERNMENT
OF CHINATOWN

Each association is, in principle, independent. Serious disputes, particularly among the large associations, could result in con-
tinuous, unresolvable fighting affecting the peace of the whole community. In order to avoid such conflicts, most Chinatowns in the
United States have established an umbrella organization. In New
York, the Chinese Consolidated Benevolent Association serves that
purpose. Its name in Chinese translates simply as Chinese Public
Assembly Hall.

Despite its name, the Chinese Consolidated Benevolent Association is structured like a government. Its most recent constitution,
drafted in 1949, declares it to be "the supreme organ of all Chinese
in New York and the neighboring states."[7] Its officers include a
president, an English- and a Chinese-language secretary (responsible
for correspondence and interpreting), a treasurer, and an auditor.
There is also a General Assembly and an Executive Council.

The CCBA has declared its right to tax its members. According
to Section 5 of its constitution, "all Chinatown businesses pay monthly
dues," varying from fifty cents to two dollars, depending on their
size. All Chinese laundries pay yearly fees of two to four dollars. All
Chinese restaurants "inside and outside Chinatown" pay yearly fees
varying from four to sixteen dollars. In a footnote, the constitution
further explains that should any restaurant or laundry miss these
payments, the organization will "forever seek repayment, and the
new owner on the premises will take over the debts."

Even more interesting is Item 6 of the same section. It states that
"all Chinese who live in New York and neighboring states must pay

a port duty of three dollars on leaving for China. Exemptions are given only to poor, aging individuals who have written explanation from their respective associations." The constitution also requires all Chinese to register their businesses and pay a foundation fee for their business locations. The CCBA can deny them recognition by refusing registration if the location is too close to a similar business or if it infringes on the interests of a powerful association. In this sense, then, the CCBA has the final say as to whether a small business can operate.

All these rules were once effectively enforced. In the 1920s and '30s the income from the fees was so substantial that the CCBA president acquired a large fortune. In fact, even recently, during elections of CCBA officials, individual kiu lings have been accused of buying votes. Today, many of the fees are no longer enforceable. However, businesses in the heart of Chinatown still pay monthly dues to the CCBA. During traditional festivals and on special occasions, the organization can still order contributions.

TAXATION WITHOUT REPRESENTATION

While the CCBA insists that it represents all Chinese, few have the right to participate in electing its officials. For instance, the president, often referred to by outsiders as the "unofficial mayor of Chinatown," is nominated for a two-year term alternately from one of two organizations, the Ning Young Association and the Lian Chen Association. Ning Young is the district association representing Toishan, and Lian Chen is the association representing all those who are not from Toishan. Until 1960 more than half the population in New York's Chinatown was from Toishan. The Toishanese therefore could claim a share of representation equal to all others. However, only the self-appointed leaders of family, village, and tong groupings could join these two associations, which have no more than one hundred members each. In the past, such a small number of people could not possibly represent all Chinese. To make such a claim today is even more absurd. Also, the Lian Chen Association, which is supposed to represent all non-Toishanese, has been controlled by members from Hsin-hui and Hok-san, two villages near Canton. They have assumed dominance because they were the two largest groups in Chinatown after the Toishanese. What this means is that fewer than three hundred people, who are mostly from three counties in Kwangtung Province, monopolize the officer positions of the CCBA.[8]

The General Assembly is the most representative organ of the CCBA. It is made up of the leaders of the sixty certified participating associations.

Today at least half a dozen of the sixty associations are defunct. Their mailing addresses and phone numbers are not in any directory. At the same time, there are more than two hundred associations and organizations which are excluded; a number of them, such as Local 23-25, the Chinatown section of the International Ladies Garment Workers Union or the Chinatown Planning Council, are larger than most of the organizations on the certified list.

The powerful Executive Council is also exclusive. It is controlled by seven permanent members, more popularly called the "Seven Major Overseas Associations." They include representatives from Ning Young and Lian Chen (the two district associations mentioned earlier), Hip Sing and An Leung (the two largest tongs), the Kuomintang (KMT, the Nationalist Party of China), Ming Chi Tang (a small, now practically defunct pro-KMT party), and the Chinese Chamber of Commerce. This was a complete range of the most powerful traditional organizations in 1949, when the CCBA constitution was drafted. Once this group of seven agrees on an issue, it has the power to make any decision stick.

The CCBA is clearly not representative of the community, nor is it a mediating force among associations. It is a body created by the largest associations, it is arbitrary and nondemocratic, and it exists to enable a self-appointed elite to maintain control of Chinatown. Designating the leaders of the most powerful seven associations as permanent members on the Executive Council was clearly intended to concentrate power in the hands of the Toishanese, the tongs, the conservative political parties, and the largest business interests.

In short, the overall Chinatown informal political structure, centering on the CCBA, is based on clans, regional associations, and tongs. It is structured so that larger traditional associations control Chinatown's governing process. And most important of all, due to an unstated policy of non-intervention by U.S. government officials, the informal structure maintains order in the community: once there is a consensus among the leading organizations, their decisions become law. For example, a few years ago the CCBA decided that the community should protest the city's closing of the local police Fifth Precinct. An order went out; every store in the main Chinatown area was closed, and 20,000 Chinese turned out for the demonstration. As a result, the city government quickly rescinded the decision.

ASSOCIATION VS. CLASS DIVISION

In each association, power is concentrated in the hands of factory owners, merchants, and landlords. Through their official positions, they are able to impose their personal interests on their associations. When all of them gather in the CCBA, they comprise an informal government, representing the interests of an elite. The community may be divided vertically along lines of kinship, village ties, trades, and fraternities; but the political structure divides it horizontally, concentrating power in the hands of the wealthy.

A 1962 editorial in the Chinese-language *Mei Chou Daily* contended that the elite had the following characteristics: they were not American-born, they were over fifty years of age, they were married and they had children (it is important to remember that before the 1940s only individuals entering America as merchants could bring their wives with them).[9]

The class nature of the social system is apparent. The class unity

of the leaders from different associations has been expressed over
the years by their indifference to issues concerning Chinatown's
working people. In the 1930s, during the Great Depression, the
CCBA refused appeals to provide relief for the unemployed. As a
result, a number of Chinese starved to death. When others formed
the Chinese Unemployed Council, the CCBA condemned it as unnecessary and Communist-inspired.[10] In 1933, when Chinese hand
laundries were attacked by white competitors, the laundrymen appealed for help to the CCBA, the only organized force in the community. The CCBA did nothing.

Today, it remains silent on the most serious problems affecting
the working poor. When the local Gouverneur Hospital, which had
served thousands of Chinese poor and elderly, closed during the
New York City fiscal crisis in the mid-1970s, the CCBA did not
protest. But when the local police precinct was about to close for
the same reason, the CCBA acted immediately to protect local merchants. Today, when the community is being ravaged by housing
problems, the CCBA offers no assistance. Instead, it supports local
merchants by demanding city funds to pay the youth to clean Chinatown's streets each summer.

ETHNIC SOLIDARITY
OF THE ELITE

Although indifferent to the problems of the poor, Chinatown's elite promotes an official ideology of the community, its
version of ethnic solidarity, i.e.: "We are all Chinese and we should
not fight among ourselves." The ideology is proclaimed during labor/
management disputes. "We are all immigrants in this country, trying
to make a living. If we fight, we will lose our businesses to the whites
and all of us will suffer."

The corollary: Chinese have their own way of resolving conflicts.
Chinatown does not need outside intervention, and more to the
point, a Chinese should not seek outside legal recourse in case of a

dispute. It is commonly understood that until all internal means are exhausted, residents will not resort to the American courts.[11] Those who break the code of silence will be punished. The case of a woman who worked in a Chinese-owned, unionized garment factory is typical. She complained to her union representative about management's violation of union work rules. The following week, ads including her picture were placed in several Chinese newspapers. The caption said: "This is So-and-so, who is a good worker but is unhappy working at such-and-such a factory. Would some kindhearted owner please hire her?" She was effectively blackballed.

The purpose of the code of silence is to prevent residents from obtaining help from the larger society. Under the informal political system, working people will not get a fair settlement: in a labor/management dispute, the Chinese elite will side with management. However, when the establishment itself is threatened, the code of silence is not binding; the CCBA might turn an opponent over to the Immigration and Naturalization Service or to the police; the elite monopolizes the community's access to the outside world. The idea is simple: let outsiders know only what the elite wants them to know.

This dominance of the elite is strengthened by their ability to control the Chinese-language newspapers. Most papers depend on revenue from local advertising. Repeatedly, associations have ordered their members to withdraw advertisements whenever a news story was not to their liking. The result is self-censorship; the press stays away from controversial issues. At the same time, most Chinese reporters, particularly the younger journalists, are susceptible to appeals of racial pride and ethnic solidarity. In recent efforts to unionize restaurants, the press has consistently taken a neutral stance—the "We're all Chinese" argument.

The CCBA has a monopoly on Chinese culture and tradition. Over the years, it has used appeals to tradition to enhance its authority. It obtained money from the Taiwan government to erect a statue of Confucius as a Chinatown landmark, and each year the CCBA organizes an official celebration of Confucius's birthday.

CCBA: CORRUPT AND INCOMPETENT

With its organizational and ideological power, the CCBA has been able to control Chinatown. However, those who have risen to leadership have not been very competent. Energetic, innovative, and open-minded individuals are too threatening to win a leading position in the CCBA. The president has to be able to wheel and deal in traditional ways. More than anything, he has to endear himself to the older kiu lings. Few chosen for the post are knowledgeable about American society; indeed, they need not be. Individuals who prosper in this circle rarely have a firm command of the English language. The president who served during the 1984–85 term could hardly speak a word of English, nor could he read the language.

While leaders may not be competent in dealing with the larger society, many are expert in defrauding their own community. They have been known to line their pockets with the fees collected from residents. They have also used their positions to support their private interests. In the early 1960s, a major fund-raising effort was launched to build a new CCBA headquarters. Years later, the president has yet to give a full account of thousands of dollars in missing funds.[12] In 1983, the CCBA borrowed almost $2 million to rescue the failing Chinatown Day Care Center. There are still unanswered questions about how much was borrowed and in whose name the loan was transacted. According to a document produced by the United Orient Bank, the signers on the loan represented a previously unknown organization, the Chinese Community Center, whose officials were totally different from the CCBA's.[13] It is not even clear whether title on the day-care center belongs to the CCBA, even though it is still making a hefty monthly mortgage payment on the property.

TONGS IN
CHINATOWN

Corruption aside, the most notable failure of the CCBA over
the years has been its inability to resolve conflicts among the major
associations, along with its inability to control the tongs. Worse, the
tongs have at times even controlled it.

For decades Americans knew about the existence of Chinatowns
only through news stories about tong wars. Those sensationalized
accounts of "hatchet men" played on stereotypes. As for the law-
enforcement authorities, tongs are discussed in the same breath with
the Italian Mafia and other organized-crime groups. While a great
deal has been said about tongs, few Americans understand them.
They are not very well understood even by the Chinese: some claim
that tongs are mutual-aid merchants' associations, some say they are
secret patriotic organizations, others consider them nothing but
criminal groups.

The origin of the tongs was actually quite benign. The word "tong"
means simply chamber. The organization was patterned after secret,
patriotic societies, the Triads, which formed some three hundred
years ago in China to overthrow the foreign rule of the Manchus
(the Ch'ing Dynasty) and restore the Ming Dynasty. In the course
of centuries, the Triads have changed a great deal and spread worldwide to Chinese communities, particularly in Hong Kong and in
Southeast Asia. They were introduced to North America during the
last century, about the same time as other family, village, and trade
associations. Tongs, however, were started in the United States by
individual members of small and weak clans who did not want to
be pushed around by the powerful and prestigious Lees and Tams,
or by the Toishanese.

Since members of a tong were not related, they pledged allegiance
to one another as "brothers in blood oath." Their bonds were further
strengthened through mystical, religious rituals, a secret language,
and signs. The code of loyalty and the pledge to revenge any wrongs
committed by outsiders against a fellow member represented the

highest virtues for tong members. Violence was necessary for self-defense; thus, there was a need for a highly organized military force within each tong. Soldiers, called "Brave Tigers," were at the core. In fact, one had to become a soldier and prove oneself before moving into the leadership ranks. On the West Coast at the end of the last century, these soldiers were known to use hatchets as weapons; hence the term "hatchet men."

Of course, violence was not used by the tongs alone. All the associations considered violence a necessary last resort to resolve conflicts. Most of the major associations had fighters ready to use force to defend their collective interests, to expand their territory, or to maintain their monopolies. The associations engaged regularly in armed combat, but only the tongs enjoyed a distinct advantage in these situations. Anyone could join a tong, but membership was kept secret. So in any battle with tongs, members of an ordinary association would not always know their enemy and its strength. The element of surprise gave the tongs a clear edge. Regular association members began to join tongs for extra protection, as insurance; they could rely on the "professional" soldiers of the tongs to fight their battles. Eventually everyone became affiliated with a tong. Conflicts which had originated between regular associations were fought out among the tongs. In effect, tong wars reflected deep-seated conflicts in Chinatown; the inability of community institutions to resolve problems peacefully resulted in tong wars.

At the turn of this century, intense competition developed in New York's Chinatown, due to the increased Chinese migration from other parts of the country. Conflicts among associations could not be resolved, and the CCBA was powerless to restore order. Battles, occurring intermittently for almost twenty years, took the form of tong wars. Outsiders had the impression that the conflicts involved a small number of tong members, who in reality were only the paid soldiers in wars fought by proxy.

Indeed, there was a criminal side to tong activities. As soon as New York's Chinatown took shape in the 1880s, the tongs cornered gambling, opium, prostitution, and other illegal trades. They catered to the weaknesses of isolated, lonely, single males in the community. In some cases, tongs did not operate these illegal businesses but extracted protection money from those who did. Tongs would battle among themselves over disputed territories. For instance, when Chinese prostitutes were smuggled in from China, tong wars frequently erupted over the control of their earnings. Illegal operations swelled the tong's coffers. When a tong became powerful and secure in a particular territory, it extended protection to regular businesses by extorting payments.

Tongs provided immigrants without education or skills with a channel for rapid social advancement: criminal activities. However, not everyone in a tong was involved in illegal pursuits. Some members joined because they could not find protection elsewhere. Except for the powerful people at the top and the soldiers who fought the battles, most tong members were peaceful residents who joined simply to avoid harassment. But once a large number of residents were members of tongs, the community's standards in dealing with problems were reduced to the lowest denominator: might is right. And as violence stimulated more violence, the atmosphere of the whole community was poisoned.

In considering the criminal aspects of tongs, we must appreciate the social environment in which they arose. Tongs became a major force only when the informal political structure of Chinatown failed to resolve problems peacefully. From this perspective, then, it is understandable why there was little stigma attached to joining a tong. For example, a few waiters I know belong to a powerful tong. They immigrated to this country recently and work in a restaurant located in the tong's territory. The restaurant owners are tong members, and the top tong bosses frequent the establishment. These bosses treat everybody working in the restaurant as their "subjects"; they are friendly but paternalistic, and the waiters feel that they enjoy a special relationship with the tong. In order to be secure in their jobs and to continue a cordial relationship with the powerful, the waiters decided to join the tong.

Tongs have always been a force in Chinatown. They have had

large memberships, they have had sources of income to finance their
standing soldiers, and they have been feared. Their power became
recognized when the two largest tongs, the Hip Sing and the An
Leung, were designated members of the Seven Major Overseas Organizations of the CCBA. But it was understood that the president
of the CCBA would not be selected from their ranks. However, the
informal political structure of Chinatown has given official sanction
to the tongs; they have become part of the establishment, though
nobody wants to announce that fact in a public meeting.

THE CCBA AND THE KUOMINTANG

While the CCBA and the traditional associations are not popular, nobody has been able to do much about them. In the past,
particularly before the 1960s, public criticism was rare. In the mid-
1930s, the editor of the *Chinese Commercial Times*, Y. K. Chu, became
so incensed with the corruption of the CCBA that he wanted to tell
the world about it. But he was afraid the CCBA would organize a
boycott of his paper, so he wrote a book entitled *Chinatown Inside
Out*, under the pseudonym Gor Yun Leong. I interviewed Chu in
the late 1970s, just a few months before he passed away, about events
that had taken place some forty years earlier. I also confronted him
with the authorship of the book. He readily admitted it, but asked
me not to make it public, because he was still active in the community.

Part of the reason people feared the CCBA was that it had acquired
influence outside Chinatown. When federal authorities needed to
deal with a community, they went to the top, to the recognized
representative of the ghetto, to the CCBA. The CCBA president's
claim of being the unofficial mayor of Chinatown was supported by
the larger society's ready acceptance of the designation.

In the past, and until recently, the legitimacy provided by the
Chinese Nationalist government was more important to the CCBA,
because sojourners who did not intend to stay in America continued

to see the government of China as the real authority. Thus, in the past, many overseas identified China's fortunes with their own and attributed their mistreatment in the United States to the low status of their homeland. They wanted to see a stronger China, and so overseas Chinese were particularly patriotic. They consistently have shown extraordinary concern for the welfare of their homeland and have contributed, both spiritually and financially, to strengthen China.

When the Kuomintang government consolidated its power in 1927, it recognized the political and economic importance of the overseas Chinese. The new government set up an Overseas Affairs Bureau in 1928, under the direct command of the ruling KMT (Nationalist) Party. The KMT was pragmatic: it wanted to ensure that it would receive the continued financial support of the overseas Chinese, particularly the regular remittances to families in China. Chinatown residents were also seen as investors in Chinese industries. And so the party tended to cultivate relations with the wealthy, influential elite in Chinatown.

Internally the Nationalist government followed a conservative path. It established a one-party system, contending that the Chinese were not yet ready for democracy and needed a period of political tutelage. All opposition, including labor unions and other mass organizations, was suppressed. The ruling party soon consisted chiefly of Mandarin officials who represented the economic interests of landlords and capitalists.

The Nationalist government also carefully watched events in the Chinese communities overseas. It opposed left-wing elements to prevent any opposition in overseas communities to government policies. The KMT did not try to politicize the overseas population on Chinese domestic issues, but it encouraged them to be patriotic and to preserve traditional Chinese culture.

To realize these objectives, the KMT since the late 1920s has allied itself with the establishment of Chinatown, i.e., the traditional informal political structure. The main task of the Chinese consulate in New York was not issuing tourist visas but maintaining the support of the local community. In fact, the criterion for choosing the Consulate General was his ability to speak the Toishanese dialect. KMT officials were regular guests at the CCBA functions and those of other associations.

For its part, the Chinatown elite were pleased to have earned the KMT's official recognition. It strengthened their authority in the community; they had an ally in suppressing local opposition. Moreover, they could attack their opponents in the context of Chinese national politics. This alliance of the CCBA, the traditional associations, and the KMT was an alliance of shared ideology and politics. Each represented the interests of an elite against labor militancy, liberal sentiments, and mass movements. The CCBA, in a way, became an extension of the KMT. The KMT Chinatown branch joined the power elite in Chinatown, and remains one of the permanent members of the CCBA Executive Council and one of the Seven Major Overseas Associations.

POLITICAL HEGEMONY

One important tool used by the CCBA and the KMT to dominate Chinatown is the Chinese-language press. For Chinese immigrants, news from China has always been important. However, the small Chinatown population made it difficult to sustain daily newspapers. The KMT understood this and has always funded newspapers of its own in American Chinatowns. The government's policies and its interpretation of world events could be presented in these papers. While independent Chinatown newspapers faced constant financial problems, the KMT-sponsored papers usually had the largest circulations, because they could afford to charge low subscription rates. These papers also presented the official position on events in the Chinese communities; the power of the CCBA, the KMT, and the traditional associations over Chinatown was not only organizational but also ideological.

There has never been a successful challenge to the elite's control of Chinatown, although the Chinese Hand Laundry Alliance did build a strong opposition in the 1930s. During the Great Depression, conditions for the Chinese were harsh. The nonresponsiveness of the Chinatown establishment forced many residents to find their own solutions. There were at the time some two thousand small, mostly individually operated, Chinese hand laundries in New York City. The operators formed a broadly based, professional organization outside the CCBA to fight for their livelihood. With the help of liberal American lawyers and political activists, the CHLA was able to moderate the city's racial ordinances against Chinese laundries and reduce the unfair advantages held by white-owned laundries. The alliance became the rallying point for increasing numbers of other Chinese workers, unions, and political activists. With its democratic method of organization, the CHLA was emerging as an alternative community leadership to the CCBA.

The traditional associations became alarmed and started sabotaging the work of the CHLA. They forced their own members who had joined the CHLA to resign. Then they started a red-baiting campaign. The KMT sided with the CCBA, accusing the CHLA of being Communist-controlled. Members of the CHLA, being more liberal, tended to be critical of the Nationalist government's policies, particularly of its unwillingness to fight Japanese aggression in China during the 1930s. As a result, the CHLA leaned toward the views of the KMT's opposition in China, including the Communists'.

In 1937, when the KMT formed a united front with the Communists against Japan, the CHLA became involved with the American forces, which were sympathetic to China's struggle, and urged the U.S. government to take action against international Fascism. The Chinese in New York, under the leadership of the CHLA, joined the CIO and the National Maritime Union in demanding that America end shipments of scrap iron to Japan.[14] The CHLA and other liberal Chinese organizations also joined a coalition of American activists, including movie actresses, in a parade on Fifth Avenue, urging women not to buy stockings made from Japanese silk.

When the United States declared war on Japan in 1941, the Chinese for the first time were allowed to work in American defense-related industries, and Chinese seamen who shipped out on Liberty ships delivering supplies to European allies were given membership in the National Maritime Union.[15]

The stranglehold by the CCBA and the KMT on Chinatown was broken after World War II because of the extreme unpopularity of the Nationalist government, which fought a civil war against the Chinese Communists right after a long war with the Japanese. Moreover, despite millions of dollars in aid from the United States, the Chinese economy was on the verge of collapse. In China, people who were not necessarily Communists were fed up with the Nationalists and wanted a change. Similar sentiment existed in Chinatowns in America. What also angered overseas Chinese was the KMT's manipulation of exchange rates, so that money sent home was worth several times less than its real value. The recipients in China suffered, and government officials made millions in the process.

Near the end of the 1940s, the prospect for change in Chinatown was bright. Chinese were beginning to break into American industries and unions; they were increasingly accepted in American society. The power of the KMT and, by extension, its ally, the CCBA, was on the verge of collapse. The CHLA and other new, independent organizations were emerging to replace the old order. But there would be no change.

Political attitudes in Chinatown were influenced by the American role in the cold war. As the leading Western power in the postwar years, the United States viewed the growing strength of the Communist bloc under the Soviet Union as a major threat to the free world. In 1947, America intervened in Greece under the Truman Doctrine, and the cold war between East and West began. There was a wave of investigations of Communists in the government by the House Un-American Activities Committee. Hundreds of careers were destroyed. More than two million government employees were required to submit to the loyalty-oath program in order to combat the "Communist menace" in America.

The U.S. government backed Chiang's Nationalist regime, even after it was driven off the Chinese mainland to the island of Taiwan.

American support for Taiwan intensified in the early 1950s, when the army of the People's Republic of China engaged American troops in a bitter confrontation in Korea. In the eyes of diehard anti-Communists, Chiang Kai-shek could do no wrong. Since most residents of Chinatown showed little support for Chiang, U.S. authorities automatically assumed that they were pro-Communist. Some Chinese Americans were accused of being Communist agents: subpoenas were issued, investigations conducted by the FBI, and deportation orders handed down by immigration officials.

These developments greatly altered the political environment of New York's Chinatown. The KMT and the CCBA were rejuvenated. Riding the wave of anti-Communism, the KMT and the traditional associations turned to red-baiting to attack their opposition. They formed the Chinatown Anti-Communist League, which any group that wanted to keep out of political trouble was quick to join. The CHLA refused to join and became an outcast; its members were harassed by the Justice Department and the Immigration Office; its influence in the community was destroyed. The KMT also attacked the *China Daily News*, an independent paper with anti-KMT views, by warning all stores and laundries "not to advertise in the Russian *Daily News*."

AMERICAN INTERVENTION IN CHINATOWN POLITICS

Historically, the U.S. government had been "passive" in dealing with affairs in Chinatown. However, this was not the case in the 1950s, when the KMT and CCBA's anti-Communist stance coincided with the views of U.S. authorities. In 1951, government officials rounded up eighty-three Chinese in New York suspected of being Communists.[16] Many were deported or forced to return to China. Most of the CHLA leaders came under investigation on charges of illegal entry into the United States. Members of the Chinese Youth Club, an anti-KMT group, were constantly harassed, to the point that few dared to remain members. The editor of the *China Daily News*, Eugene Moy, in April 1952 was summoned to testify before a grand jury in the Southern District of New York for possible violation of a U.S. code—the "Trading with the Enemy" Act. The paper had allegedly accepted advertising revenue from the Bank of China.[17] Later, in 1954, a court found Moy guilty; he was fined and served a one-year term in Danbury State Penitentiary.

By the mid-1950s, the CCBA and the traditional associations, with the assistance of the KMT and U.S. authorities, regained control of Chinatown. The community had been terrorized into submission: fearful of being labeled Communists, residents shunned politics. Once again, the CCBA, the traditional associations, and the KMT monopolized the political arena. Every October the CCBA organized a demonstration in front of the United Nations to oppose the admittance of the People's Republic of China. The CCBA claimed it represented "Chinese popular sentiment the world over." Until the early 1970s no organization in Chinatown dared to display the People's Republic's five-star flag. Insofar as the CCBA was concerned, it alone represented the community's view. And insofar as outsiders were concerned, all Chinese Americans were anti-Communists.

TONGS, GANGS, AND THE GODFATHER

6

TODAY, the informal political structure in New York's Chinatown has to contend with a totally new situation. Most residents are recent immigrants from urban centers in Asia who have no previous connection with traditional clan and kinship organizations. The Chinese Consolidated Benevolent Association no longer commands unlimited authority, because the KMT has lost both credibility and power, particularly since the normalization of relations between the United States and the People's Republic of China.

Furthermore, the community is no longer isolated from the larger society. Government agencies provide a variety of services in Chinatown: from senior-citizen centers, mental-health clinics, free English-language instruction, to drug counseling. Immigrants depend less on the traditional associations; they can go directly to government agencies for assistance. More and more, disputes are settled in U.S. courts. In fact, so many Chinese are turning to the courts that city officials face a serious shortage of interpreters. Younger, college-educated Chinese American activists are bringing a new political consciousness into the community. As a result, residents are more outspoken and better informed about their rights.

A key factor contributing to the weakening of the old informal political structure is the impact of new money. While the CCBA used to regulate the old Chinatown economy comprised of self-employing small-service trades, it holds little sway over new manufacturers, developers, and real-estate speculators with overseas capital.

One would expect that these new economic forces would spell the demise of the old political structure; most Chinatown residents look at the CCBA and the traditional associations with indifference, even contempt, believing them to be phenomena of the past which will soon disappear. However, one should not rush to conclusions.

There are still forces in Chinatown that want to see at least parts of the old order preserved. The associations are still attracting a following, due to the wealth of these organizations. Every major traditional organization still owns its own building. These buildings are located in the core of Chinatown and are worth a great deal at today's real-estate values; they also generate tens of thousands of dollars in rental income each year.

The KMT government in Taiwan continues to woo the kiu lings, giving them legitimacy and financial support. The president of the CCBA and top association leaders are made members of the Chinese Nationalist government's Legislative Assembly with handsome yearly salaries.[1] On every "Double Ten Day" (10/10), the national day of celebration, a delegation of kiu lings is given a free trip to Taipei. Also, the Taiwan government has regularly awarded them exclusive rights to import Taiwanese mushrooms and canned goods. Finally, the government, to this day, continues to give contributions to the traditional organizations.

The old informal structure operated effectively when Chinatown was an isolated community. While many now may not respect the CCBA and the traditional associations, some profit by having Chinatown remain an entity separate from the larger society. For some businessmen, the isolation of Chinatown limits outside competition and protects ethnic markets. For certain employers, the isolation allows them a monopoly over Chinese immigrant labor.

But how can such an enclave be maintained with so many diverse interests? This is where the advantages of the old informal structure become immediately apparent: it is there, ready to be used, with existing institutions and leadership. Even though it has been weakened, its associations still have members, and they still own property. So far, no equivalent political force has emerged; the CCBA president is still recognized as the unofficial mayor of Chinatown. In other words, among the weak, the old structure is still the strongest.

Today, physical force or the threat of it is the most effective method for the elite to command compliance. It is therefore not surprising that tongs have grown in power, increasingly competing for leadership within the informal political structure. The power of the tongs is not absolute, but the power structure within new Chinatown is so very delicately balanced that any force with extra resources may become dominant.

The fortunes of the tongs have had their ups and downs. Tongs become active when Chinatown experiences rapid expansion and different interests in the community cannot resolve disputes peacefully. This was the case between the 1910s and the 1930s in New York. Many old-timers still remember the horrors of the tong wars, when residents were forced to stay indoors, and businesses came to a standstill. Homes and storefronts were barricaded. Children attending public schools had to be protected by armed guards employed by the tongs.[2] By the early 1930s, the wars were out of control; battles spread from San Francisco to Boston. The Chinese embassy in Washington sent a first secretary to New York to propose a peace treaty between the Hip Sing (United in Victory) tong and the An Leung (Peaceful and Virtuous) tong. They refused. The general public became outraged at the senseless violence that threatened innocent American bystanders going about their business in the vicinity of Chinatown. In 1931, the New York City Police Commissioner and the U.S. Attorney called in leaders of the Chinese community. They were threatened with deportation and then forced to sign a peace agreement. The tongs gradually disarmed, but they quietly continued to operate their illegal activities.

The end of fighting may have been influenced partially by the drastic curtailment of immigration, thus lessening the competition and economic pressure. From the early 1930s to the late 1950s, Chinatown enjoyed peace without major tong wars. Young people were no longer involved in fighting. It was during those years that Chinese youth got the reputation of not having any juvenile-delinquent problems. This, of course, was not true, but the statistics did suggest a very low rate. At least, the youth problems in Chinatown during those years were not related to the tongs.

However, this peaceful situation ended with the rapid increase in immigration in the 1960s. Violence and organized crime escalated almost in the same proportion. Youth gangs reappeared. The tong-inspired gang wars started again; there were killings almost weekly, and the situation became so serious that the local police and the district attorney's office each set up a special task force to deal with it.

THE TONGS' NEW IMAGE

Today everyone inside the community realizes that the tongs are behind the gangs, but nobody dares to point a finger. Tongs, in the meantime, have worked hard to reform their image. An Leung no longer calls itself a tong—it is now the An Leung Merchants' Association; the former Hip Sing tong is now known as the Hip Sing Public Association. However, they have not changed. Just as Manhattan District Attorney Robert Morgenthau asserted in a recent public statement, Hip Sing and On Leong (An Leung in Cantonese pronunciation) are both tongs involved in protective associations with youth gangs which serve as enforcers, controlling gambling, drug dealing, and extortion of the city's Chinese community.[3] Both try to give the impression of being engaged exclusively in legal businesses. Hip Sing operates its own federally insured loan association. An Leung rents part of its headquarters building to the United Orient Bank, established with money from Taiwan. The bank has representatives from the An Leung Merchants' Association on its board of directors.

The elimination of "soldiers" from their organizations is the most important change. Today tongs sponsor youth gangs who are not members of the tong; they subcontract the dirty work to these gangs. A tong pays a coordinator to recruit and organize a gang. This coordinator, or *dai low* (elder brother), is ideally a charismatic martial-arts instructor or ex-gang member from Hong Kong who is able to command a faithful following of young toughs. Gang members follow orders from the dai low and have no relations with the tong. All communication, including money and instructions, is between the dai low[4] and a middle-level tong official, the "contact."

Every dai low guards this communication link as his exclusive role within the gang. The advantage to the tong is that only two people are directly involved; unless they talk, the relationship between the tong and the gang cannot be proven. Even if they knew the details of the connection, gang members would not talk, lest they be eliminated as traitors.

The gangs protect gambling houses, deal in drugs, extort money from merchants, and collect loans and protection money from theaters, nightclubs, and massage parlors. They are also used to intimidate and silence the opposition.[5] Gang members are provided with apartments, money, and cars. They go around the community demanding respect from everyone. They may walk into a local restaurant, order a large banquet, have a member sign the check, and walk out. This is called "eating a tiger." When they need money, they enter a store and ask the cashier, "*Ah-sok* [uncle], can I borrow some money? I'm kind of short."

Most of these youths are between the ages of fourteen and seventeen; they are eager and fearless. When they are provided with guns, gang members know that no one will cross them or report them to the police; when they are caught, they are quickly bailed out and given full legal assistance. Even though local residents and the police know that the tongs are behind the gangs, they also know that gathering evidence against the system would require a major and dangerous effort.

Since the 1950s, specific gangs have come and gone. First there were the Continentals, who were mainly second-generation Chinese Americans. Later, gangs were usually comprised of immigrant youth, who are considered to be tougher. Most notorious are the Black Eagles, the Flying Dragons (once, the Hip Sing fighting force), and the Ghost Shadows (at one time the An Leung's force).[6] In the 1980s new gangs have mushroomed; there are the Tun-an, the Golden Star, the Chung-i, the White Tigers, the Fu-ching, and the Hung-ching. Probably most feared today are gangs organized by Vietnamese immigrants of Chinese descent.[7]

The gang relationship to the tongs is not difficult to see, even for an outsider. For instance, a few members can always be seen standing guard in front of tong headquarters or at the doorways of gambling houses. Also, there are the extortion operations in Chinatown. In most stores and restaurants there is a framed, printed certificate in Chinese stating that such-and-such tong appreciates the store's generous contribution to its charity fund drive. This is displayed prominently, usually on the wall behind the cash register. This puts other gangs on notice that the premises are already protected.

THE NEW GODFATHER

Tongs allow recruitment of new members without regard to kinship or place of origin. With an unlimited constituency, tongs are able to undertake many different activities. They are able to adapt to modern conditions. Precisely for these reasons, tongs are taking full advantage of the weakened CCBA and moving into leadership positions in the informal political structure.

Chinatown's most interesting figure in the 1980s is Benny Eng, the "Permanent Advisor" of New York's Hip Sing tong. He is popularly known as Uncle Seven, Chinatown's version of the Godfather. Mr. Eng is over eighty years old and a gentleman who seems to understand that in order for the informal political structure to maintain power, it has to reach out to the Chinese beyond traditional institutions. His first step in the 1980s was to change the image of his tong, from that of a feudal, sectarian organization to one concerned with problems of the entire community.

He projects himself as a responsible, civic-minded leader who speaks for the common people. His theme is consistent: Chinese should be united and work together to solve their problems. To show his conviction, he has often acted as a mediator between feuding groups. For instance, a few years back the community-run Chinatown Day Care Center went into bankruptcy because of mismanagement. The Chinese Consolidated Benevolent Association and a Chinatown social-welfare agency both fought for control of the center, but neither was willing to take responsibility for its debts. They tried to work together. A long-drawn-out dispute developed because of their inability to agree on a joint list of members to sit on the center's board of directors. There were bitter charges and countercharges. Finally, Uncle Seven stepped in. He first negotiated with several Chinese-owned banks to provide the center with a highly favorable mortgage; he then pledged to contribute $5,000 a month toward running the center.[8] Finally, he mediated between the warring sides to work out a satisfactory list of board members. Actions like these have won him praise from all sides.

Part of the negative image of the old political structure was its ultraconservative, anti-Communist position. Uncle Seven also tried to change that. In 1984 S. B. Woo ran as a candidate for lieutenant governor of the state of Delaware. His campaign was significant because he was the first East Coast Chinese to seek a major elected post. Woo, an immigrant from Hong Kong, toured Chinese communities across the country for financial support. The first group to respond enthusiastically was the Fukienese Association in New York City, since Woo is Fukienese by descent. However, because the association is known to be openly pro-People's Republic of China (it is one of the very few traditional associations to display the five-star Chinese flag on October 1, National Day), KMT elements in Chinatown branded Woo as a leftist and urged others not to support him. Uncle Seven thought otherwise. In a well-publicized statement to the Chinese press, he labeled those critical of Woo as narrow-minded people still wasting time on the politics of China. "When we are here," he said, "we should get involved in American politics and be united in building a new future in this country."[9] Once he had spoken, all the different groups came out openly in support of Woo.

In the past, taking such a controversial position would have been political suicide, for almost all traditional associations maintain close ties with the KMT. But when Uncle Seven spoke, nobody contradicted him. Even the KMT kept silent. At the 1984 Hip Sing annual convention, the head of the Taiwan Coordinating Council for North American Affairs in New York (the equivalent of the consulate general from Taiwan) dutifully bowed to Uncle Seven during the public ceremony.[10] On Mr. Eng's birthday, Taiwan's President Chiang (the son of Chiang Kai-shek) sent him a personally inscribed scroll. Uncle Seven's statements have so pleased the People's Republic that it sent a special delegation from Peking to attend the National Convention of Chinese Freemasons (Hung Man Tong), chaired by Uncle Seven.

With such power and prestige, he eventually carried out a major coup for the tongs. He repeatedly criticized the CCBA for being too restrictive and undemocratic—a criticism supported by the vast majority of Chinatown residents. Eventually, the General Assembly of the CCBA met in 1986 to amend its constitution, allowing tong members to run for office. Thus, an almost century-old CCBA rule was changed. Uncle Seven's efforts finally gave the tongs legitimacy, and a tong member could very well be the next CCBA president.

In the early morning of December 22, 1982, four masked gunmen with automatic weapons broke into the Golden Star Bar on East Broadway, the hangout for members of the Freemasons, and started shooting. The gunmen escaped in a waiting car, leaving three people dead and eight seriously wounded. One of the dead was only thirteen years old. It was one of the worst massacres in New York City's recent history.

That morning, after a meeting with their leader, Herbert Liu (Liao in Mandarin), forty remaining members of the Freemasons, fully armed, marched to the headquarters of the Hip Sing tong. They challenged the Flying Dragon gang, whom they accused of having committed the murders, to come out of the building. Fortunately, the Flying Dragons did not come out. Liu was not appeased and called a news conference, accusing Uncle Seven of being the Godfather of the Flying Dragons gang and masterminding the killings (Benny Eng denied all responsibility).[11] He further announced his willingness to testify on these charges in court. The police proceeded to provide him with the full protection accorded a star witness in the grand jury investigation of the massacre.

According to insiders, Liu had been a member of the Hip Sing tong but was now interested in developing an independent operation on East Broadway, a new area of Chinatown's expansion. The tongs at the time had not yet agreed on who would control the street. Liu, without the permission of the Hip Sing, started his own gang and set up a gambling operation in a basement on East Broadway.[12] He was repeatedly told by Hip Sing leaders to stop, but he refused to do so. Weeks after the massacre, the Hip Sing tong published a statement: "Herbert Liu, a member of our Association, has repeatedly violated Association rules by forming gangs and disturbing the peace of the community. After deliberation, members of our association have unanimously voted to expel him from the organization. . . . We will not tolerate any group trying to protect him or interfere in this matter."[13]

Liu never testified against Uncle Seven. Instead, he issued a public apology. However, this apology did not end the killings. In March 1983, the leader of the Flying Dragons, Michael Chen, reputedly a close associate of Uncle Seven, was murdered. The Hip Sing tong, in fact, posted a $10,000 reward for information regarding Chen's murderer.

These events seem not to have affected Uncle Seven's prestige.

This is partly so because the local Chinese papers have not published anything unfavorable about him. For instance, in late 1984, the President's Commission on Organized Crime made several references to Uncle Seven's alleged crimes. All the Chinatown papers, with the exception of one, blacked out the news. The ensuing general silence in the Chinese press made it appear as though these events never occurred. And Uncle Seven's reputation has continued to grow. As a matter of fact, the 1985 Convention of the National Organization of the Chinese Consolidated Benevolent Association in North America elected Benny Eng its Honorary Permanent Chairman.

YEAR OF THE DRAGON

While Uncle Seven was trying to project a different image of the tongs, Eddie Chan was trying to transform his tong into a modern organization capable of financial growth and participation in American politics. His was a most ambitious and incredible ascent to power.

Previously, he had been a police sergeant in Hong Kong. When the colony established the Independent Commission Against Corruption, Chan and several other "suspected" police officers left for Taiwan.[14] Chan emigrated to this country from Taiwan in 1975.

He had enough money to purchase a couple of restaurants in Chinatown, a funeral parlor on Mulberry Street, and part-ownership of a Chinese movie-theater chain. Soon after his arrival, Chan became a powerful force in the An Leung tong; he was quickly elevated to the position of executive director.

Eddie Chan's unusual, rocketlike ascent to prominence may have inspired Robert Daley, a novelist and an ex-deputy police commissioner of New York City, to use him as one of the main characters in his novel *Year of the Dragon*.[15] The hero of the novel is an eccentric Irish cop; the villain, an ex-Hong Kong police officer, Mr. Koy, who owns a funeral parlor in Chinatown. Through the struggles between these two antagonists, the book dramatizes the international Chinese crime network and the role of local Chinatown tongs. In the novel, Koy organizes a group of ruthless youth into a gang, intending to take total control of Chinatown. Then he uses his membership in the Triad, a worldwide Chinese secret society network, to master-mind the smuggling of heroin from the Golden Triangle in Southeast Asia through Amsterdam to New York. Once in New York, the drugs are distributed by Koy's Mafia connections.

Although Daley's book is fiction, the characters and events seem true to life. In addition to the similarities between Koy and Eddie Chan, there are other characters whose identities Daley did not try hard to disguise. Niki Louie, the famous leader of the feared Ghost Shadows gang, allegedly the fighting arm of the An Leung tong,[16] is named Nikki Han in Daley's novel. In the opening chapter there is a description of an assassination attempt on the mayor of China-town; in 1978, there was just such an attempt on the life of M. B. Lee, then the president of the CCBA.

Daley, as a high Police Department administrator, had access to records of investigations into Chinatown crimes, and his "fictitious" indictment of Koy should stimulate readers to ask some serious questions. Is there any truth to the existence of a Chinese Mafia? Are the Chinatown tongs really part of a growing international crime network? A few residents understood the implications of Daley's novel, but the Chinatown press totally ignored it.

Daley's book was published in 1981. If he thought politics in Chinatown were interesting then, the situation since has become even more intriguing. Chan's real-life adventures are much more exciting than any writer could imagine. He either has been very successful in his businesses or has had access to overseas money from Taiwan and Hong Kong. Whatever the case, he has become a major shareholder in one of the first privately owned, overseas Chinese banks in Chinatown. The United Orient Bank on the Bowery opened in 1981, with Chan as vice chairman. By 1983 the bank added another branch on Mott Street, in the An Leung headquarters build-ing. Matilda Cuomo, the wife of New York's governor, cut the ribbon at the grand opening and spoke at the banquet that followed.

Chan has also been very active in community affairs. He was made an elder and an advisor to the An Leung tong. He took control of the Chinese Welfare Federation "to fight for the rights of Chinese Americans in this country";[17] as its president, he lobbied in Congress for further liberalization of the Chinese immigration quota and rallied Asian American communities to stage a national protest against racial discrimination, centering on the case of Vincent Chin, who was killed in Detroit by two Americans, an unemployed auto worker and his stepson, who mistook him for Japanese. These activities gained him high visibility; the Chinatown press depicted Chan as a model, civic-minded leader.

As if these activities were not enough, Chan has entered the American political arena, where traditional Chinese associations have long been weak. Because of the low voter turnout in Chinese communities, most American politicians ignore Chinatown during elections. At best, they pay a quick visit during the campaign, to have the television cameras show them shaking hands with the mayor of Chinatown or eating an egg roll in front of a Chinese crowd. Otherwise, politicians do not usually campaign for the Chinese vote. As a result, they owe nothing to the Chinese.

Eddie Chan, on the other hand, has money. As a self-proclaimed Republican, he contributed to the Reagan/Bush re-election campaign in 1984. He has also contributed to the campaigns of local Democrats, including Geraldine Ferraro, the late Queens borough president Donald Manes, Congressman Mario Biaggi of the Bronx,[18] and Mayor Koch. These contributions, as well as his political lobbying in Washington on Chinese American issues, have made Chan a leader of the Chinese people. The Chinese community regularly saw pictures of Mr. Chan in the local Chinese papers, posing with prominent American politicians. For a recent immigrant, Chan has come a long way. His is a true American success story: from beginnings as a humble public employee in Hong Kong to celebrity status in this country, with money, connections, and respectability, all in a very short time. His questionable past and even the publication of a damaging best seller did not seem to hurt him at all.

During the hearings on Asian crime by the President's Commission on Organized Crime in October 1984, Chan's name was mentioned in several of the sessions. Chicago detective Joe Carone and Drug Enforcement Administration agent John Feehan testified that Eddie Tse C. Chan had been identified by two informers as a major Chinese organized-crime figure whose organization in 1980 dispatched eight members of a New York street gang to Chicago to assassinate a dissident gang leader.[19] He was also accused of initiating new members of the Ghost Shadows in ritualistic Triad ceremonies.[20]

The commission's staff investigator, David Williams, also testified that Chan was a former Hong Kong detective sergeant who immigrated to the United States during a Hong Kong investigation of police corruption. He said that in 1983 a high-level Triad leader in Hong Kong identified Chan as an organized-crime figure and gang leader in the United States.[21] Williams also charged that Chan was a major figure in an international commodities swindle that bilked millions of dollars from Chinatown waiters, homeowners, and cooks, as well as from businessmen from Hong Kong and elsewhere.

Both the *New York Post* and the New York *Daily News* followed the revelations of the commission hearings with a number of investigative articles focusing on Mr. Chan's dealings with local politicians. In the meantime, the commission requested Chan's appearance. He refused, and avoided talking to the American press, but he did grant interviews to local Chinese reporters. There were people, he claimed, who were trying to discredit Geraldine Ferraro during the presidential election campaign by slandering him. If the charges against him were true, he said, why was he cleared by the Immigration and Naturalization Service when he applied for citizenship, and again by the Liquor and Tobacco Control Commission, which granted his restaurants liquor licenses? Chan insisted that he was a law-abiding businessman, and that the public recognized him as such. He had been honored by the Republican Party, invited to be a member of the party's inner circle, and appointed chairman of the Reagan/Bush Re-election Chinese American Voters Registration Subcommittee.[22]

Although Chinese-language papers sent reporters to the hearings and several papers reported the testimony on the front page, most papers avoided naming local individuals who were targeted by the commission and did not use this opportunity to expose evidence of organized crime in Chinatown. Their silence was due in part to reporters being told not to "tarnish the image of the Chinese."[23] Several days after the hearings, articles and editorials in Chinese-language papers argued that the presidential hearings had been scheduled as a media event right before the national election; that the hearings did not produce "solid and convincing" evidence against individuals such as Chan; and that while criminal elements did exist, the testimony exaggerated the extent of their activities.

THE TONGS' PRESENT OPERATION

To suggest that the extent of crime in Chinatown is exaggerated is absurd. Anyone who reads the local papers will find that not a week goes by without reports of gang killings. When thirteen- and fourteen-year-old boys carry guns and shoot each other in daylight on crowded streets with hundreds of witnesses, none of whom will testify in court, the problem is serious indeed.

Some people claim that crime is simply a youth problem. They complain about the quality of today's youth, blaming the schools and the corrupting influence of American culture. They even try to give sociological excuses, seeing the problem as the result of the generation gap or the failure of hardworking parents to spend enough time with their children. Yet this problem is not simply one of juvenile delinquency brought on by parental neglect or bad schooling. When jobless fourteen-year-olds have guns, apartments, spending money, and defense lawyers for protection, they obviously have the backing of powerful adults. The youth problem is the creation of the tongs.

But one still hears that the situation with tongs has been exaggerated, that tongs are dying organizations run by conservative old men who don't amount to much. If there is still any doubt about the tongs' real involvement in community crime, here is the list of currently known tong operations in New York City:

1. There are at least five gambling houses in Chinatown open twenty-four hours a day. Hundreds of working people go there to place bets. *Fan tai*, poker, and Thirteen Points are the most popular games. Since each bet may be twenty to thirty dollars, a gambler can easily lose several hundred dollars per visit. Every one of these houses takes in thousands of dollars each day. All of them pay protection money to tongs, and hire their gang members as bouncers and gambling-debt collectors. According to the police, the proceeds from these gambling operations are used to maintain the youth gangs.[24]

2. According to the police, tongs extort protection money from 50 percent of Chinatown's stores.[25] In the heart of the community, the percentage is higher. The extortion operations have spread outside of Chinatown to Chinese-owned stores throughout the city and its suburbs.[26]

3. In the heart of Chinatown, different tongs claim territorial control. They must approve new businesses in this area. In 1985, a group of investors bought a restaurant inside the sphere of influence of one tong. The tong forced the parties to break their contract because the new buyers were not members. Another group of buyers, who did belong to the tong, eventually acquired the restaurant.

4. Chinese-owned movie theaters, nightclubs, massage parlors, and bars are targets for extortion, even when they operate outside Chinatown. Unless these operations have solid backing from a powerful tong, they are not likely to be left alone.

5. There are weekly reports of youth gang break-ins at Chinatown garment factories and wholesale seafood and dry-goods warehouses.

The tongs act as fences, helping to dispose of large quantities of stolen goods without detection.

6. According to the police and federal authorities, tongs are involved in drug trafficking. Several Chinatown banks are suspected of helping to launder the drug money.[27]

It is understandable that some people in the community understate the problems with tongs. They live and work in the community and have nowhere else to go. When confronted with criminal threats, they have to be practical. That's why so many businesses pay protection money. It is cheaper to pay a few hundred dollars a month than to have one's storefront window broken or to worry about the safety of one's family. Once people have accepted this situation, they become used to the tongs' existence. So when outsiders talk about the tongs, many residents become annoyed to the point of accusing them of exaggerating the problem and talking only about bad things in the Chinese community.

When Robert Daley's book *Year of the Dragon* was turned into a Hollywood action movie, critics did not like it because of its excessive violence. Daley did not like it either and disclaimed any connection with the movie. Asian American activists and a number of community leaders organized pickets in front of the movie theaters and urged a boycott. They condemned the movie as sexist and racist, and said it tarnished the image of Chinese communities. The last objection is unfortunate. Clearly the tongs are a serious problem, yet the community is "kept silent," and is powerless to stop them. Only when the public is fully aware of the facts will pressure be put on government authorities to act against the tongs. To block public exposure under the pretext of opposing stereotypes plays into the hands of the tongs.

GUNS FOR HIRE

Tongs are not just involved in crimes; their impact on the community is far greater. In today's polarized Chinatown, they are particularly dangerous. They can be hired by anyone willing to pay. One restaurant union organizer complains: "Every time we get somewhere with our unionizing effort, some tong member who claims to be an old friend of the management will approach and suggest that we not push his friend too far and make him lose face, if we want to avoid unnecessary bloodshed among us Chinese." In one case, when the restaurant owner discovered that the waiters were planning to unionize, he hired a well-known Taiwan gang leader with close tong connections as his manager. In garment factories, individuals who complain too much about working conditions are often threatened. So long as workers are not able to act as a group, these threats will be effective. Even where workers understand their rights and want to report unfair labor practices to the union or to the National Labor Relations Board, they end up dropping the matter, because they fear physical retaliation by the boss's hired guns.

Once workers are intimidated, management is free to violate basic labor rules without worrying about government interference. So the problem with the tongs is not limited to the crimes they commit; they impose a class structure on the community as well, buttressing the power of employers. The passivity of government authorities in dealing with tongs has not only forced the community to live in fear, it has also helped to perpetuate an economic structure which violates customary standards.

The COMMUNITY
AND GOVERNMENT
INSTITUTIONS

7

CHINATOWN is plagued by a series of problems, crime and housing being the most serious. But the existence of an exploitative economic system, backed by the power of a traditional informal political structure, is more fundamental. What is the prospect for change?

THE ROLE OF GOVERNMENT INSTITUTIONS

Government officials have not taken appropriate action to meet the community's pressing problems. The way that law-enforcement authorities deal with the tongs is indicative of the attitude of the other branches of government as well. Why aren't they enforcing the law and cracking down on the tongs?

The usual response is that the authorities are doing all they can;

the problem lies with Chinatown residents who are not cooperating. The authorities complain that the Chinese do not report crimes, even when they are victims.[1] On May 19, 1985, during lunch hour, a group of young gang members pursuing another gang rushed into a busy restaurant and started shooting. Seven people were wounded, a four-year-old boy and a white customer among them. Hundreds saw the incident, yet no witness came forward. The Southern District's assistant district attorney in charge of monitoring Chinatown organized crime, Nancy Ryan—nicknamed "the Dragon Lady" by the Chinese community—complained to the Chinese press that during her nine years on the job few Chinese had cooperated with her investigations. She contended that it was precisely this reluctance that allowed gangs to become uncontrollable. She maintained that by refusing to testify against another Chinese, residents were not in fact supporting "ethnic solidarity"; their silence harmed the community and damaged the image of the Chinese.[2]

However, Chinatown residents who were interviewed after that shootout looked at the situation quite differently.[3] To them, the problem lay with the police, who were not doing enough about the gangs. Despite many gang killings, the community rarely hears of convictions. It is known that the local Fifth Precinct has set up a Jade Special Task Force to deal with Chinese youth gangs. And it is also known and admitted by the task force that it has the names and photographs on file of all known gang members. One shop owner wondered aloud: "Why don't they do something about them?"

The situation with gambling is similar. It is not that difficult to locate gambling parlors. One can easily spot them just by casually walking around Chinatown. Several are in basements on Mott Street. On the days when they are operating, there is usually a sign in Chinese reading HOI-P'EI, announcing that games are going on. In 1984, a newly appointed Fifth Precinct captain promised the community that he would eradicate gambling in three months. Because the income from the gambling houses provides the funds to maintain youth gangs, closing them down would cut off funds to the gangs. Gambling establishments were raided, dozens of individuals arrested, thousands of dollars and gambling paraphernalia confiscated. The raids made the headlines of every newspaper. For a short while the houses were closed, but just a few months later, it was business as usual.

This was nothing new. Much of the community is downright cynical. Many are convinced that the police have been paid off. According to a persistent rumor, "inside" cops inform the gambling establishments about plans for raids, so that the owners can be prepared. In fact, there are Chinese reputed to be "professional prisoners," i.e., those paid to stay behind when a police raid is anticipated. They are booked, locked up overnight (in the Tombs, within earshot of Chinatown), and released the next day after being admonished by the judge. Two different Chinatown reporters interviewed these prisoners and estimated that they were paid between fifty and one hundred dollars per night.[4] And the police could take credit for "enforcing" the law.

Thus, the unwillingness of residents to cooperate with the police is not surprising. It's one thing to report a crime, but it's quite a different matter to have to continue to live and work in the community after doing so. Residents' criticism of the way the police handled the kidnapping case of a twelve-year-old girl illustrates this problem.

Mr. and Mrs. Liang I-An, who both worked in garment factories, returned home after work one day to find their twelve-year-old daughter missing. Later, they received a phone call demanding twenty thousand dollars in ransom. The Liangs reported the case to the police. Since their son was known to be a member of a youth gang, the police suspected rival gang involvement. Without consulting the Liangs, the Fifth Precinct initiated a major search, broadcasting information about the missing girl from loudspeakers mounted on police vans. The police asked for information and help. The precinct captain also called an emergency news conference. At the same time, the police, through informants, demanded that known gang members cooperate in the search or face arrest.

Twelve days later the girl's body was found dumped in the back of a tenement building. The father was outraged and contended that the extensive police publicity had caused the kidnapper to panic and murder the girl. After a meeting with the president of the CCBA, Liang at a news conference threatened to sue the Fifth Precinct for gross negligence in the handling of the case.

A Hong Kong "girlie" magazine, similar to *Playboy*, carried a critical piece about the incident. The article, written by a New York Chinatown reporter who wanted it published in Hong Kong, where such kidnapping cases are common, showed how poorly the New York police had handled the case. The writer maintained that the police should have established contact with the kidnapper in order to gain time and then find ways to apprehend the criminal. His argument may be disputed, but it is clear that neither the writer nor the community trusts the New York police.

Solving the organized crime problem in Chinatown will not be easy. Residents expect the police to do more, but the police argue that the community is not cooperating. At this stage, the community is at a disadvantage. Residents are caught in the middle between the tongs and the police. The tongs' threat is real: their gangs intimidate the public, they control the community's informal political structure, and they have powerful leaders on their side who are praised in the local press and who hobnob with American politicians. In order to resist the tongs, the residents must be certain that the city authorities will stand solidly behind them. Moreover, the authorities must show that they intend to get to the heart of the problem, i.e., to eliminate the power of tongs. Thus, the initial step in dealing with crime must come from government authorities. Once firm steps are taken, the residents will be far more willing to cooperate.

Recently there have been several indications of change. Most interesting is the case of the United Orient Bank. During the President's Commission hearings discussed earlier, the community press avoided mentioning Eddie Chan. Yet news of the hearings spread throughout the community by word of mouth. It was followed by the rumor of Mr. Chan's imminent arrest, with the implication that his assets would be frozen by federal authorities. In early November

1984, after the hearings, there was a run on the United Orient Bank. Thousands of nervous Chinese depositors lined up in front of the bank waiting to withdraw their money. At first bank officials told the depositors not to panic, since the bank was insured by the FDIC. That did not help. Only when the bank announced the resignation of Chan as vice chairman and after depositors had withdrawn $6 million did the run on the bank stop.

Since 1985, federal authorities have launched several operations against the gangs. In early 1985, just days before the Chinese Lunar New Year, the U.S. Attorney for the Southern District in New York City handed down indictments against twenty-five members of the Ghost Shadows gang. They were charged with eighty-five counts of extortion, robbery, murder, and kidnapping—for crimes committed since 1971. The arrests were the result of a ten-year investigation.[5] The prosecution of gang members with bizarre nicknames such as "Fish Eyes," "Winter Melon Head," "Itchy Ass," "Stinking Bedbug," and "Horse Tumor" brought relief to Chinatown. Hundreds of federal and local law-enforcement officers were involved in the roundup. A news conference was called to make a formal announcement of the arrests. It was a major media event, with U.S. Attorney Rudolph Giuliani present. It was the first time that the federal authorities had prosecuted Chinese gangs, and it was done under a provision of the federal Racketeer Influenced and Corrupt Organizations Statute (RICO).

Still, the community's response was ambivalent. Some questioned why the Ghost Shadows were indicted for crimes they had committed such a long time before. The gang had disbanded after the arrest, several years back, of its charismatic leader, Niki Louie. Others doubted that the federal and local authorities would persist with the prosecution of other Chinese organized-crime figures. Restaurant and shop owners complained that many new gangs had already approached them for protection money.[6] Above all, most residents knew that the tongs were the real problem. Arresting gang members is not enough.

Nevertheless, any federal action against the gangs is helpful. According to reports from the district attorney's office, several of those arrested have told the police about the workings of crime networks. This may lead to indictments of more important figures in the hierarchy, even the tong leaders.[7]

Since the New York tongs are experiencing difficulties in controlling the gangs they have created, they are in a weakened position.[8] Evidently several gangs have grown so strong that they have decided to work independently. Tongs have had to recruit new gangs to crush the rebellious, thus creating more violence and continuing warfare. In addition, since 1983 a number of new gangs have arrived from other Chinatowns looking for "employment."[9] There are now more gangs than there are tongs to be serviced, adding confusion to the already chaotic underworld scene. Some of the gangs have had to set up territories uptown or in the outer boroughs.[10]

Still, the secret societies of tongs pose special difficulties for government investigators. To be effective, any government action must be coordinated at the local, state, and federal levels, requiring a major commitment of manpower and resources. Even with the RICO statute, the new weapon for dealing with tongs, government agents must work painstakingly to set up surveillance teams, search for witnesses, compile records and testimony, and make extensive arrangements to protect witnesses.

Unfortunately, dealing with tongs is still not a national priority, because most Americans are ignorant of the problem, and victims within the community remain silent. Without organized community pressure, without a clear articulation of the problem, public opinion will not be mobilized to force government officials to act. Under these circumstances, to count on the government to solve Chinatown's crime problem—and other problems—is not realistic.

NEW POLITICS

Government social agencies serving Chinatown are products of the civil-rights movement of the 1960s; they were created in response to the militant demands of racial minorities for justice and for social programs to meet their needs.

These agencies have introduced a new political dimension into the community. They provide services to residents previously provided by the traditional associations, and have brought changes that have slowly eroded the political monopoly of the informal political structure. Power in the community has slowly been diffused and decentralized. Social-welfare agencies are clearly a threat to the old order.

The Chinatown Planning Council is seen by the traditional organizations as the greatest threat. It is the largest social-welfare agency in Chinatown, with an annual budget of $12 million, and it provides job training, employment, legal aid, and mental-health services, as well as English-language classes. It operates day-care centers and a string of facilities for youth and senior citizens; it sponsors low-income-housing projects and develops income-generating nonprofit service and rental operations. The council's programs are constantly expanding to meet the needs of both recent and earlier Chinese immigrants; it has offices in Queens and Brooklyn, where new concentrations of Chinese have emerged.

The council was established in the mid-1960s, when Chinatown experienced a serious economic squeeze: the already stagnant laundry and restaurant trades were unable to absorb the rapidly increasing labor pool created by the liberalized immigration laws. The founding members of the council, mainly second-generation Chinese professionals, were disenchanted with the indifference of the Chinatown establishment. Their initial efforts during the 1960s to win a share of federal, state, and city funds were fruitless. Anti-poverty programs had just been created, and outsiders did not consider Chinese communities to be in need of help. It took persistent lobbying, even demonstrations, to convince officials in the various agencies that Chinatown residents indeed suffered poverty and desperately needed assistance.

THE POLITICS OF ANTI-POVERTY AGENCIES

The Chinatown Planning Council has since acquired a reputation for managing quality programs with a dedicated staff. Its basic approach has been to identify problems, then look for available funding. The council is financed by hundreds of individual public and private grants. The main sources of revenue are city, state, and federal programs. Day-care centers are funded by the New York City Agency for Child Development. Its senior-citizen centers are funded under the Federal Older American Act.

The Planning Council, like most social-service agencies, has to modify its programs to fit the money available. Most funding is in the form of "soft grants," designated for specific tasks; the budget is lean and designed for only one-to-three-year periods. As a result, the council has limited flexibility. On the other hand, the issues that concern different agencies change often; a few years back, drug-rehabilitation programs were popular; later, programs for the homeless were emphasized; after that, programs to deal with family violence were increased. The result is a lack of continuity. Old problems don't often go away. Some funded programs are not tailored to existing needs, and funding is not available for pressing problems.

At times, the funding sources are expedient, makeshift, and hardly appropriate. For instance, the council's youth program, Project Reach, is funded, odd as it may sound, by New York State's Addiction Services Agency. But gangs—not addiction—are Chinatown's biggest youth problem. Project Reach did claim at one time to be providing a gang-rehabilitation program. But when the White Eagles and the Black Eagles started hanging out at the youth center and provoking fights, the program collapsed. Since the mid-1970s, Project Reach has provided an after-school center for "nonviolent" youth, and more recently, it has devoted resources to a remedial English-language program for newly arrived youth from the People's Republic.

However, the Chinatown Planning Council is not an agent for

sweeping political change; it cannot challenge the Chinatown elite economically or politically. It cannot do anything about the tongs. It cannot interfere with the way landlords operate, nor can it settle labor disputes. The council provides programs to help, not to change.

Despite its limitations, the Chinatown Planning Council is seen as a serious threat to Chinatown's informal political structure: the very notion of accepting outside funding to provide social services discredits the associations' "benevolent" functions. Moreover, the council's linkage with a variety of government agencies undermines the power of the Chinese Consolidated Benevolent Association.

With the council's relationship to government bodies, the CPC has emerged as a political force in the community. It applies for funding to different branches of the government, which has the power to decide what programs are to be supported and implemented. The CPC does not have an independent position—it acts as the agent for the American authorities.

To obtain government funding, the CPC has over time developed contacts with various outside agencies and with local politicians; in recent years, it has been particularly close to Mayor Koch's administration. These relationships help it to survive and grow. For its part, government authorities can count on the CPC's support within the Chinese community.

The most political part of the CPC is its board of directors. The majority of the thirty or so members are second-generation Chinese professionals: bankers, lawyers, landlords, and appointed local government officials. They are hardly representative of the community, but because of their position with the CPC, politicians in the larger society cultivate them as consultants on Chinatown affairs. Several board members have been active in Democratic Party politics. At election time they help set up campaign committees in Chinatown for their favorite candidates. They are rewarded with appointments to community boards and commissions of local agencies. No wonder the CPC board of directors has attracted a number of ambitious Chinese, even though many have little knowledge of or contact with the community. In fact, local resident critics refer to them derogatorily as *juk-sheng* (the "heart of a hollow bamboo stick"), implying that American-born Chinese often lack Chinese soul. They cannot even hold a meeting in Chinese. But they are articulate, and they sound like insiders when they discuss Chinatown's problems with outsiders. Above all, they know the American political system, how to take advantage of it, and are adept at using the CPC to advance their careers. These appointed leaders are in a position to influence government policies toward Chinatown.

The CPC's influence on the community goes well beyond dispensing social services. On the most critical community issue, housing, the CPC has taken controversial positions, often in conflict with the residents'. Mayor Edward Koch's long-standing goal has been to revitalize New York by attracting corporations, financial institutions, and wealthy residents to Manhattan. Tax incentives and zoning changes have encouraged new construction for this purpose. At the same time, powerful economic forces are slowly squeezing out manufacturing industries, small businesses, and low-income residents; many have moved to the outer boroughs or out of the city altogether.

In Chinatown the social fabric of the community is being destroyed. Several groups are lobbying community boards to apply zoning restrictions on upper-income high-rises; they have turned to the courts to challenge construction permits. A broad coalition has gradually emerged to stop the gentrification process.

The Chinatown Planning Council has given no support to these protesting groups. Several board members have stated that it would be futile to fight the escalation of Chinatown real-estate values, and that construction of high-rises to replenish the dilapidated housing stock should be permitted. In the meantime, the council has been promoting the decentralization of Chinatown. It recommends that garment factories, businesses, and residents should move to "satellite" Chinatowns in Queens or Brooklyn, where rents are lower. In the meantime, the council itself has received grants to expand its branch offices in Queens and Brooklyn to facilitate the anticipated growth.

Many in the community are extremely suspicious of the council's intentions, because the most powerful forces on the board of directors are landlords and bankers, who are using the CPC to outflank community opposition. In 1985 Virginia Kee, a founder of the CPC and a powerful member of its board, ran unsuccessfully for the Democratic nomination for the New York City Council. She comes from an old Chinatown family with substantial real-estate interests, and as a member of the local Community Board, Kee consistently advocated giving permits for high-rise construction in Chinatown. More specifically, she lobbied for the Special Manhattan Bridge District Resolution, which relaxed the existing zoning regulations to allow construction of buildings of more than seventeen stories. She had the endorsement of Mayor Koch, because her opponent, Miriam Friedlander, who had served on the City Council for twelve years, was one of the most outspoken opponents of the mayor's gentrification programs. During the campaign Kee avoided discussing housing issues, stressing only that she was the first Asian American woman to run for elected office in New York City. But she failed to attract enthusiastic support from the Chinese community despite her ethnic appeals, and she lost.[11]

The Chinatown Planning Council is drawing increasing criticism. Because of recent cuts in federal funding, the CPC, like most nonprofit organizations, is seeking new sources of income. In addition to tapping private foundations and staging fund-raising banquets, it has set up a development office to raise capital from nonprofit—but income-generating—operations. In the last few years, it has been very successful in acquiring several nearby city-owned income-producing buildings. In all cases, the council was able to take control of these buildings with the support of City Hall. This has led to charges of unfair politicking from other Chinatown social-welfare groups and traditional associations.

In 1981 the City of New York decided to build an extension to the city prison, the Tombs, in the square block between Mulberry and Baxter Streets. Some saw the building of a prison in Chinatown's front yard as a racial affront. Businessmen, particularly real-estate agents, saw it as a barrier to Chinatown's expansion to the east. A coalition of groups opposed the project, and the city then proposed a compromise: using the lower floors of the new prison as a senior-citizen center and for other community uses. The precise location of each service area was to be determined by a community board.

The Chinatown Planning Council, with the backing of city officials, stacked the fourteen-member community board of directors to gain a controlling majority. The chair of the board was the president of the Chinatown Consolidated Benevolent Association. He did not speak English, and his role was relegated to calling the meeting to order; he sat silent during the proceedings, and then adjourned the gathering.

In the initial meetings of the board of directors for the Sung Park Senior Citizen Center, it was decided to rent the best locations on the lower floors to the Chase Manhattan Bank, the Sino-American Bank, and to several large businesses. The rest of the space was reserved for CPC programs. A coalition of community groups challenged the board's decision.

The Committee of Concerned Citizens of Chinatown contended that with high real-estate values pushing out small businesses, the board should allocate space for the latter, not banks and large corporations. However, the board remained steadfast and soon announced its decision to offer a large section to the Post Office. It was later revealed that a CPC member on the board of directors owned the old post-office space in Chinatown. As the landlord, he was suspected of having better plans for the use of his space in the heart of Chinatown. After a long battle with community opponents, the board agreed to change its policies; it then proceeded to allocate space for a few small businesses, charging them high fees as "seed money" for construction purposes. Again the community coalition protested; critics maintained that seed money without a promise of refund was illegal. The board resisted the demand that it redraw its building plans.

By then, the senior-citizens-center board had become deadlocked. The CPC lost its majority control during an underattended board meeting, when the allies of the Chinese Consolidated Benevolent Association voted to include more members on the board, including the Hip Sing and An Leung tongs and the KMT Party.

Why had the Chinatown Planning Council been so intent on

controlling the senior-center board? Some suggested that it had to do with its goal of generating income from the project for its programs.

Although the CPC has developed political influence quickly and is striving to become the leading organization in Chinatown, residents remain highly suspicious. Critics assert that the CPC, which has no constituency in the community, is not dependent on the community for survival; thus, it has taken positions favoring outside political forces, and worse still, it has sided with real-estate interests against the broad-based community coalition.

But the real failure of the CPC and, for that matter, most other social-welfare agencies is their inability to deal with the major community problems: crime, the housing shortage, low wages, and sweatshop conditions. Nevertheless, the political power of these organizations continues to grow.

THE CHINESE AND THE AMERICAN LABOR UNIONS

8

SINCE the mid-1970s, classes in Chinatown have polarized, and exploitation of workers has increased. So far, social-service agencies have not helped workers deal with workplace problems. Union organizing, it would seem, is the logical alternative.

Although working people constitute the overwhelming majority of the population, they are poorly organized and politically weak. There are dozens of merchants' associations of all types, but not a single traditional organization has formed around workers. In fact, the very idea that workers should organize into unions that cut across clan, village, and trade lines is an alien concept. At the same time, American labor unions, partly because of their racial attitudes, are unwilling to break into Chinatown to help develop a workers' movement. Thus, by 1987 less than 2 percent of Chinatown restaurants were unionized. And while most of the garment workers are members of the International Ladies Garment Workers Union, management is still able to get away with sweatshop conditions.

UNIONS IN
CHINATOWN

Chinatown before the 1960s was not fertile ground for labor organizing. Most Chinese worked in small service-oriented laundry and restaurant trades, and were either self-employed or partners in proprietorships invariably formed by people originally from the same clan or village in China. When workers were needed, they gave preference to fellow clansmen. Furthermore, the skill required in these trades was so minimal that there was no division between masters and apprentices. This gave these establishments a cooperative character: while normal capitalistic development creates a definite distinction between owners and workers, Chinese firms did not usually differentiate between employer and employees.

Small businessmen realized that survival depended on successful competition with larger, modernized, white-owned firms. For instance, white-owned laundries during the 1930s made major breakthroughs by introducing washing machines and large automatic steam presses, often operated by low-paid black or immigrant female labor. Chinese laundrymen attracted customers by providing extra services, such as free mending, free pickup and delivery, and low prices. As a result, there was constant friction between the modernized laundries and the small Chinese hand laundries, always with racial overtones. Further, the Chinese laborers developed little affinity for other American workers, and viewed unions as a threat, since the survival of Chinese firms depended on keeping costs down and wages as low as possible.

In the 1930s, at the height of the American industrial labor movement, some Chinese were exposed to American radical movements and labor attempted to organize unions in Chinatown. Except for attracting some members into the welfare-relief-oriented Chinese Unemployed Council during the Great Depression, they made few inroads. In 1935 a Chinese leftist organization, the Chinese Anti-Imperialist Allliance, recruited twenty restaurant workers into the Restaurant and Food Production Union, a branch of the International Labor Union, but these individuals worked neither in China-town nor in Chinese restaurants.[1] However, at that time, the New China Restaurant, which was located outside Chinatown, near City Hall, was the only Chinese restaurant organized by an American union, the Cafeteria Employees.

LABOR AND THE CHINATOWN ESTABLISHMENT

Today, the composition of the Chinatown work force has changed. With the expanded economy and the development of man-ufacturing industries, there is a large working class and serious di-vision between labor and capital. Yet Chinese workers are still not part of the larger American labor force, because they work in an underground economy with its own informal political structure. This structure has historically been dominated by property owners and merchants; in recent years it has been able to incorporate manufac-turers. Thus, on the owners' side, there is a powerful structure through which to exert control. The workers have no such counterforce.

To deter workers from organizing or being too active, owners have an effective weapon—the blacklist. Troublemakers are fired and are unable to find another job in Chinatown. Blacklisting is effective because there is no possibility of appeal, either to the traditional associations, to the CCBA, or to the media.

The Chinatown media are locked into this system. Reporters are enjoined from reporting what might stir up community conflicts. For example, in the summer of 1984, waiters picketed against the owners of the Hong Kung Restaurant on Pell Street, whom they accused of union busting. An editorial in the Chinese-language *Pěi-Měi Daily* commented: "If only both sides could sit down and ne-gotiate in good faith, and if each side would make some compro-mises, this situation could be resolved without resorting to American courts. After all, we are all the offspring of our ancient emperor

Wang-te, we have the same skin color, we speak the same language, we have sprung from the same roots; why should we be so impatient with each other? In the face of racial discrimination, which we all suffer, and relentless competition from American businesses, it is wrong to fight among us brothers."[2]

Workers in the Chinese community have no effective organization to represent them, nor a leader to champion their interests. Even federal and state authorities are not troubled by widespread violations of minimum-wage laws in Chinatown. The Department of Labor won't take any action unless the Chinese complain, and the workers cannot complain for fear of retaliation.

Under these circumstances, the only way for Chinese workers to improve their lot is through organizing. Yet the American unions have not responded. Typical is the attitude of the AFL/CIO Hotel and Restaurant Employees and Bartenders Union, which has frustrated the activism of Chinese workers.

THE RESTAURANT WORKERS UNION MOVEMENT

There are 450 restaurants in Chinatown and another thousand or so Chinese-owned restaurants elsewhere in the New York metropolitan area. Before 1978 very few Chinese restaurants were organized. The AFL/CIO Hotel and Restaurant Employees and Bartenders Union, Local 69, tended to focus its energy on expensive restaurants and hotel, hospital, and company dining rooms; because they have a large number of workers concentrated in one place, they are relatively easy to organize. The union claims that Chinese restaurants are too scattered and too costly to organize. Thus, the initiative for unionization of Chinese restaurants in New York City had to develop from the workers themselves.

In the late 1970s, there were (and still are, of course) a number of expensive and well-known Chinese restaurants on the Upper East

Side of Manhattan. The owners of these very profitable establishments, who had never worried about unions, treated their workers badly. Waiters, for instance, were paid low wages and worked long hours; they had neither job security nor benefits. It was common for management to order them to do chores that they were not hired to do, such as dumping garbage, mopping floors, cleaning bathrooms, or running errands for the owners.[3] Some establishments provided only leftover or inferior food for the workers and charged them for it. Most of the employees were non-Cantonese immigrants who spoke English and had been in this country for some years; many were over forty years old. The few who were more politically active, frustrated by their working conditions, eventually asked the Hotel and Restaurant Employees and Bartenders Union, Local 69, for help. The union had no plans to organize the Chinese, but agreed to help as long as the workers themselves assumed the responsibility. In May 1978, Uncle Tai's, a fancy Upper East Side establishment serving Szechuan food, became the first Chinese restaurant in the city in almost forty years to become organized.

Others soon followed. By 1979 workers in at least four other non-Chinatown Chinese restaurants had joined Local 69. They were organized with overwhelming support, because the workers, having accumulated grievances over a long period, had finally found a vehicle for dealing with their problems. Even so, the process of organizing was not easy, because the owners resisted fiercely. Although Local 69 had not hired professional union organizers, many Chinese waiters were so excited by the prospect of unionization that they volunteered to help.

However, the waiters who joined the union were soon dissatisfied. Local 69 regularly refused to enforce contracts and allowed management to get away with violations of labor codes. At several restaurants workers contended that Local 69 had settled for inadequate medical benefits. Members at one restaurant accused the representative from their local of sitting by while they were replaced by non-union workers.[4]

Local 69 was a typical "business union," more interested in collecting dues than in representing its members. Once a restaurant was organized, the union rarely enforced contracts aggressively, because any dispute with management would require costly litigation. Further, this type of union prefers to organize from the top down: to reach an agreement with management permitting unionization, while the union, in turn, promises lenient contract enforcement. Complaints by the workers had little effect. After all, the union had never been keen on organizing the Chinese in the first place.

In response to these complaints, union activists formed the Chinese Staff and Workers Association. It claimed to be a social club, although its main objective was to promote unionization in the Chinese community. Thus, the association worked to develop a strong voice responsive to the needs of its Chinese members. Some even hoped that eventually the union would establish a Chinese section in Local 69.

Nonetheless, the response of Local 69 was not encouraging. The case of Peng's Restaurant shows the union bureaucracy at its worst. In 1978, organizers from Local 69 approached the workers to join the union. Since the majority were reluctant, the unionization effort failed; in addition, two union supporters were fired. In 1980 the union went back again. This time, despite warnings of dismissal and threats by the owner, the workers voted 14 to 2 to join the union. So the owner closed the restaurant and reopened it three months later under a new name. The "new" owner allowed the workers to be organized by Local 69 but refused to rehire those who had voted for the union under the "old" management. The union went along with this arrangement. The old workers had to sue the new management for unfair labor practice. They won in the end—after five long years of court proceedings—but during the trial the union testified for the management.

In 1979, a whole year after the first wave of Chinese restaurants had been organized, Local 69 reluctantly agreed to hire a part-time Chinese organizer. In short order, the organizer persuaded workers in five uptown restaurants to sign up. However, the union business agents were incompetent and passive; in subsequent efforts to negotiate contracts, all the organizing efforts were fruitless. It seemed that the union did not really care. The workers suspected that some officials had been paid off by management. The defeat was bitter and cost many workers their jobs. By then, almost all the Chinese union activists realized that working with Local 69 would turn Chinese workers against unions altogether and end the growing movement.

In February 1980 a dispute broke out at the largest Chinatown restaurant, the Silver Palace. The dispute was triggered when management asked the waiters to kick in additional shares of their tips for the busboys, the business managers, and the maître d'. Customarily, a waiter's tip was divided into thirty shares, two of which went into the pool. In the Silver Palace's case, management argued that since business was so good and tips plentiful, waiters should contribute two additional shares. The waiters, who were paid less than $150 a month and relied on tips as the major part of their income, protested. Management fired fifteen of them. The waiters asked for their jobs back, but management refused and hired new workers to take their place.[5]

The waiters then approached the Staff and Workers Association for advice. After discussion, they decided to picket to force management to negotiate. The Staff and Workers Association quickly mobilized other waiters from uptown unionized restaurants along with its membership and contacts in Chinatown. Mass meetings were organized and a support committee was formed. The association headquarters on East Broadway became the command center. Fired waiters took turns on the picket line. The support committee called in union activists from around the city, so that during business hours there were forty to fifty individuals circling the front door of the restaurant. On weekends, when the restaurant was busiest, there were almost one hundred pickets. Other volunteers, including community activists, young lawyers and other professionals, wrote bilingual leaflets and issued news stories to the media. At the same time, waiters visited workers in other restaurants to explain the issues and ask for pledges of support. In almost every instance, workers from these restaurants contributed money for the strikers and their families.

Such open defiance in Chinatown was a shock to the community. Previously, union drives had taken place outside Chinatown. Many believed that organizing within the community was not possible because restaurant owners had rigid control of the immigrant work force. It was even more surprising that the workers had dared to take on the management of the Silver Palace, since it was the most respectable restaurant in the community, specializing in elaborate, large dinner parties and formal banquets. It could accommodate one thousand guests at one sitting; it was booked months in advance for important association celebrations and political fund-raising dinners, suggesting that management had powerful connections. In fact, one of the restaurant's partners was the president of the Chinatown Restaurants Association, and several others were well-known leaders of a prominent tong. In one respect, though, it was logical that the Silver Palace should be the first Chinatown restaurant to have a labor/management dispute: it employed more than one hundred workers, making it a likely place for union consciousness to develop.

The picketing severely reduced business at the Silver Palace. The community honored the picket line, because countless residents were either working, or had worked, or had close family members working in restaurants. Even some owners of other restaurants believed that the Silver Palace management was arrogant and had pushed the workers too far. The sentiment in the community for the workers alarmed the owners. Many people pressured the Silver Palace to settle quickly, and finally management agreed to rehire the strikers and to withdraw its demand for an additional share of the tips. The owners' capitulation represented an overwhelming victory for the waiters.

When the workers realized that they had won, they understood that simply getting their jobs back would not ensure job security. They needed to form a union to protect their gains and to improve working conditions. Should they join Local 69? Several heated debates were held at the association headquarters, those in favor of joining Local 69 arguing that without the backing of a large union workers would have neither the organizational nor the financial strength to protect themselves. On the other hand, uptown workers who had

had dealings with Local 69 spoke against affiliation, and the experience of the Silver Palace waiters with the local had been instructive. At the beginning of the strike, workers had approached union officials for support in their attempts to win back their jobs, but the officials refused to help unless the waiters joined their union. This only deepened the Chinese suspicion of the purely business nature of Local 69. Finally, and perhaps not surprisingly, the Silver Palace workers voted overwhelmingly (27 to 7) in favor of forming an independent union not affiliated with Local 69.

Once rehired, the waiters negotiated with management for formal recognition of their union. Although these negotiations went on for months, it was clear that management was in no position to block the union. Thus, the Silver Palace became the first restaurant in Chinatown to be organized, and its workers the first to set up an independent union.[6]

The union contract included all the basic terms and benefits guaranteed outside Chinatown: a forty-hour workweek, overtime pay, a minimum wage, health benefits, paid holidays, collective bargaining, and job security. The terms of the contract were revolutionary insofar as the Chinese community was concerned. No other Chinatown workers enjoyed anything comparable. Most of the larger restaurants in Chinatown quietly improved conditions in order to avoid unionization. Within two years, workers at three other restaurants organized independent unions.

However, after these early successes, the momentum of the independent union movement slackened. Workers had shown militancy, but in order to maintain their gains, they needed organizational strength. Since workers in each restaurant formed an independent union, the organizational base was weak. There was a loose alliance of independent unions through the Chinese Staff and Workers Association. Dues were collected to provide funds for health insurance, pensions, and strikes. However, each union had very limited resources. In cases involving expensive legal battles or drawn-out strikes, the independent unions had to turn to the Staff and Workers Association for support. The association, a voluntary membership organization, was not even able to hire full-time organizers, and without organizers, the independent union movement cannot grow, further contributing to its weakness.

Restaurants have become shrewder in dealing with unions; they sabotage organizing efforts by resorting to legal maneuvers. Stanley Mark, an attorney for the Asian American Legal Defense and Education Fund, which represents Chinese workers, observed: "We have had four cases in one year alone where owners closed the restaurants after the workers voted for unions. These places reopened months later, with new names and reshuffled corporate ownership. Usually we are able to win court cases against them, but only after long months of deliberation. By then the workers had found work elsewhere." Mark also suggested that with the Reagan Administration's anti-labor policies and the recent Supreme Court decision allowing weakened businesses to file for bankruptcy under Chapter 11, businesses can legally evade union contracts. The job security of the workers and the power of their unions in the restaurant industry have been jeopardized.

Moreover, in Chinatown management remains strong because of its institutional and ideological hold over the community. In order to counter that power, union members must go beyond the workplace; they need to join with other Chinatown residents to form a new base of power from which to address a variety of issues.

This is a difficult task, requiring time and resources. Nevertheless, the restaurant workers have dramatically changed the political landscape of Chinatown. Widespread restaurant unionization is accepted as certain. The owners' argument that unions would kill their business has been shown to be invalid: the Silver Palace since unionization is still the most popular restaurant, with prices no higher than other establishments'. Moreover, under the union contract, service has improved and the tension between management and workers has lessened. In the meantime, the Chinese Staff and Workers Association has developed into a solid, mass-based organization which restaurant workers in Chinatown can claim as their own. They come to it whenever they face problems and need advice.

The success of independent unions has pressured Local 69 (recently renamed Local 100) to improve its work in the community. The local finally hired several Chinese organizers and unionized a number of Chinese restaurants (mostly uptown). Local 100 officials have also developed a mutually supportive relationship with the Staff and Workers Association and the Chinese independent unions. On occasion, the two forces join each other's picket line.

However, problems between community activists and Local 100 continue. The Chinese Progressive Association (CPA) argued during the formation of independent unions that activists should continue to work within American unions, even if they were corrupt, in order to reform them from within. Subsequently, several CPA members were hired as organizers for Local 100. However, almost all eventually quit because of the impossible situation in the union. One CPA member and organizer became so outraged that he joined a workers' picket line in front of a unionized Chinatown restaurant in defiance of the union, which had branded the picket line as an illegal wildcat strike.

In the final analysis, Chinatown restaurant workers want the advantages of a large American union. However, the unions have not shown sensitivity to the needs of immigrants in ethnic communities, and until they do, the Chinese will not join. Chinatown garment workers, on the other hand, do have a large union behind them.

THE ILGWU AND CHINATOWN SWEATSHOPS

The International Ladies Garment Workers Union started to organize the Chinese as early as 1957. By 1974 all Chinatown garment workers had joined Local 23–25 of the union. Unlike the Hotel and Restaurant Employees and Bartenders Union, the ILGWU wanted the Chinese. Since the early 1970s Chinatown has been New York's leading center for the production of women's apparel, the city's most important manufacturing industry. While the ILGWU's general membership had declined drastically, membership in Chinatown had increased dramatically. Local 23–25, whose membership is 85 percent Chinese, has become the most important ILGWU local. In fact, the last manager-secretary of Local 23–25, Jay Mazur, who presided over its rapid expansion, has moved up to become president of the ILGWU.

The Chinese belonging to the ILGWU presumably have all the advantages that the restaurant workers in independent unions do not. The ILGWU is a national union, with a membership of over 200,000, staff and business agents in the thousands, and a large budget which enables it to organize and recruit new members and to withstand long strikes. Historically, the union has also played an influential role in the Democratic Party. In addition to its powerful political allies, it has lobbyists in Washington to support legislation beneficial to its members.

But despite all its power, the ILGWU has not yet brought full union benefits to its Chinese members. The union negotiates a new contract with Chinese management every three years, but working conditions are still well below minimum union standards. The complex piece-rate system is not enforceable, because the employers always concoct their own formula to underpay the workers. Working conditions are hazardous to safety and health. On the average, Chinese garment workers are on the job ten to twelve hours a day, six days a week, and make only about $9,000 a year. These are nineteenth-century sweatshop conditions. The only protection the union members truly enjoy are the health and pension benefits, although the union has even cut back on them, because of the decline in contributions from the contractors and manufacturers.

Most Chinese contractors have small business operations in comparison to the large union, yet they do what they want on the shop floors. Union officials have never been willing to organize an active rank and file in order to defend the workers' interests. This reluctance is rooted in the union's peculiar strategy of organizing.

UNION STRATEGY IN CHINATOWN

In the early 1970s, when manufacturers recognized the productive environment of Chinatown, they willingly signed an agreement with the ILGWU to stabilize the labor situation. Once the manufacturers took the initiative, all the other arrangements followed. The union got the most out of it, since it was able to sign up all the workers in Chinatown factories. Because of the unstable nature of the garment industry, the ILGWU prefers to organize workers from the top down. At present, the garment industry is divided into four sectors: manufacturers, contractors, the union, and the workers. The manufacturers don't manufacture anything; they provide design specifications, determine production volume, and secure the necessary capital. The contractors get orders from the manufacturers and hire women to do the work. And the union represents the workers in the contractors' factories. However, the ILGWU does not aggressively confront the contractors because, after all, they operate marginal businesses. Further, negotiations usually begin with the manufacturers, who provide the money which affects the wage scale. The union appeals to the manufacturers' desire for stable production conditions by having them award jobs only to contractors who hire union workers. So the ILGWU normally begins its organizing efforts with the manufacturers. Once the union comes to terms with the large manufacturers, it then goes to the contractors. The contractors usually accept the union's terms, because the union has commitments for work supplied by manufacturers. Finally, the union, with the approval of the contractors, organizes the workers. This organizing method may not require serious shop struggle at all. The critical point is to convince the contractors that it is in their self-interest to agree to recognize the union.

Under these circumstances, the union has divided loyalties. It represents the workers, but it also must be sensitive to the problems of the manufacturers and contractors in order to hold the whole package together. If the manufacturers and contractors were to move their operations elsewhere, there would be few jobs and fewer union members. As a result, the union moderates its demands to make sure they stay in business. In carrying out this constructive role, the union is not single-mindedly representing the workers. For this reason, it is sensitive to any movement among the rank and file which might lessen its ability to carry on its delicate negotiations. The union is centralized and does not appreciate activism from its members.

UNION LOCAL 23–25

The garment factories in Chinatown were unionized by organizing the contractors. It was the easiest, quickest, and cheapest way for the union to succeed. So women became members of the union without the experience of struggle. Once they joined, the ILGWU made little effort to establish its presence on the factory floor. In many factories shop representatives, whose job it is to take up workers' complaints with the bosses, were, in fact, chosen by the owners. In some cases the ILGWU business agents, who represent the union in overseeing individual shops, get along better with the owners than with their own members. This is not surprising, since the success of the union clearly depends more on cooperation with the contractors than with the rank and file.

Most women who work in the industry are recent immigrants with no previous union experience. Furthermore, the union local consists almost entirely of Chinese. The women are not exposed to other American workers; nor are they familiar with working conditions in other American industries. The power of management is dominant. The contractors do what they like, violating contracts at will and blacklisting those who dare to speak out. When dissident workers are fired, the union is not able to get their jobs back because the business agents regularly side with management. There have also been innumerable charges of officials taking bribes.

Formal contracts are in effect, but violations are pervasive, and the union acts as though nothing was wrong. When asked why there are so many clear violations in Chinatown factories, officials reply that the union always prosecutes these cases vigorously *if* the workers file formal complaints. Few Chinese ever do, because it is a complex and treacherous process, inviting possible retaliation from the contractors and betrayal by union officials.

The union claims that the Chinese cooperate with management by knowingly working off the books, not reporting management's cheating on piece rates, secretly working on jobs from non-unionized manufacturers, and even taking work home. On the other hand, the union has made no effort to educate its members: it prefers to emphasize the services it provides the workers. To many Chinese, the union is nothing more than a health-insurance company.

MILITANT CHINESE WOMEN

The ILGWU seems to consider Chinese women difficult to organize, because they are thought to be passive and tied to Chinatown's political and social structure. But in the summer of 1982, during the negotiation of a new contract, this stereotype still shared by so many was shattered. The negotiation involved renewal of a three-year contract and called for standard wage increases. The manufacturers signed the agreement; the union and the negotiating unit for the contractors (the Greater Blouse, Skirts, and Undergarment Association, translated as the "Foreigners Garment Merchants Association") also agreed to terms. In fact, this same contract had already been signed to cover 120,000 non-Chinese garment workers on the East Coast. Unexpectedly, all the Chinese contractors balked, claiming that the negotiating unit did not represent them, since they had not been consulted during the negotiations. They were angry because even though 85 percent of the firms affected by the contract were Chinese-owned, there were no Chinese on the negotiating team. Furthermore, Chinatown's shops were the only ones in the industry that were doing well. As the backbone of New York's garment industry, and the most vital segment of Chinatown's economy, the contractors expected the community to rally behind them, particularly in this clear instance of racial discrimination. The contractors said to the workers: "We are all Chinese and should be able to settle this in our own house; there is no need to go to the white man's union." And knowing that the Chinese women were particularly concerned about health benefits, the contractors promised to provide the same benefits if they got out of the union.

The union had not expected this roadblock; it decided to head off the challenge by a show of force. It called for demonstrations in Columbus Park, on the edge of Chinatown, to defend the contract. According to some accounts, the union leaders had no idea how the Chinese women would react to the decision, since its staff was not close to the membership. Some doubted that the Chinese women would turn out to confront their own establishment in Chinatown.

But the reaction was overwhelming. Hundreds of women volunteered help: some operated phone banks to contact individual members, others wrote bilingual leaflets, banners, and propaganda material. Shops were mobilized by militant leaders who emerged from the rank and file. On the day of the first demonstration, 20,000 workers turned out. This was a historic event. Never before had so many Chinese, much less Chinese women, turned out over a labor issue. One of the leaders, Alice Tse, a new immigrant, spoke during the rally: "We cannot accept any treatment that is inferior. Chinese workers are people, too! We should receive equal treatment. . . . This is the true eternal spirit of being Chinese! If we cooperate and stand together behind our union, we will win! Let's celebrate our coming victory! Let's celebrate our historical show of unity demonstrated today."[7]

After two demonstrations, the Chinese contractors backed off and the workers won a new contract. The militancy of the Chinese women had been the key to victory. They had not been able to act on factory floors, because they were isolated and silenced by the community's conservative establishment, which represents owners, but the ILGWU's call for mass mobilization unleashed their militancy. The critical point was that the union had shown its support for the workers, who then realized that they did not have to be passive and cooperate with management: in fact, they repudiated those who did.

For many garment workers, the events of 1982 were their first real experience with collective protest. They now saw new possibilities for improving conditions in their shops. If they maintained their solidarity, they could stop owners from violating labor codes. And if the power of the rank and file was consolidated, the union could pose a serious challenge to the community's traditional political order. Workers would then no longer fear intimidation and blacklisting.

However, the ILGWU as an institution has never been comfortable with a militant and active rank and file;[8] militant workers threaten the maneuverability of the union leadership in negotiations and the delicate balance in the industry. Many union officials have turned into career bureaucrats, concerned primarily with maintaining their jobs. Over the years, leadership has remained in the hands of white males, particularly those of Jewish origin,[9] even though the membership of the International Ladies Garment Workers Union has been overwhelmingly female; its ethnic composition has changed from Jewish to Italian, to black, to Puerto Rican; today, it is mainly Chinese and Hispanic. Although at present 85 percent of Local 23–25 members are Chinese, only in the past few years has the union opened staff jobs to Chinese; none, however, is in a decision-making position.

During the serious, closed-door negotiations in the 1985 contract talks, all the representatives of the manufacturers and contractors were male; on the union side also, there were only males. Women, who are in fact the foundation of the whole industry, had no chance to voice their concerns—their interests are still being represented by male officials who are not even aware of their own chauvinism.

After the events of 1982, the union did not use the opportunity to strengthen the rank-and-file structure at the shop level. It did not improve the training of shop representatives, it did not replace the passive business agents, nor did it institute labor-education programs for its membership. It did, however, recruit the most militant workers to join its staff; there, they could no longer organize fellow workers but had to channel their energies into "acceptable" directions. They were assigned to so many high-profile projects that members began to see them as clever public-relations ploys. For example, some of the union's staff were shown in Chinese papers demonstrating against apartheid at the South African consulate. It was a worthy cause, except that most union members at the time were more upset about the cutback of health benefits. No wonder a critic observed that the ILGWU has a complete "foreign policy" but no position on its own members.

A UNION IN CRISIS

Today, the American garment industry is in crisis. In the last twenty years clothing imports have jumped from an 11 percent to a 54 percent share of the U.S. market. Manufacturers, including those who originally signed contracts with the union, have switched their production to Third World countries and imported the finished products to the United States at much lower prices. Of the three hundred or so American manufacturers that used to provide jobs for Chinatown contractors, only about eighty are still doing so. The rest either moved their entire production abroad or contracted work out to non-union shops. Chinese contractors complain that orders from unionized manufacturers keep only 40 percent of their work force busy. And since the union is no longer able to deliver enough work from the manufacturers, contractors are demanding concessions, most specifically permission to take on jobs from non-union manufacturers. The union has refused to let Chinese contractors do so unless they contribute a high percentage of their income from those contracts to union membership funds. Violators are subject to fines.

But it is widely known that Chinese contractors, fearful of going out of business, have solicited jobs from non-union manufacturers to keep their factories busy. They are doing this without telling the union. The response from the union when it learns of these violations has been mild. In November 1985, the Department of Labor indicted five men for conspiring to evade taxes by falsifying records. The accused were owners of the Leung Family Group garment factories. According to the charges, they were accepting work from non-contract manufacturers, and in order to cover up this violation, they had the manufacturers pay them through a bank account opened under a fictitious name. Each check was to be in an amount less than $10,000, in order to evade scrutiny by banking authorities. In all, the Leung Family Group has allegedly avoided paying federal income tax and contributions for union health benefits on unreported income totaling $3 million.[10]

The Labor Department's action was the first major crackdown of its kind in the Chinese community. The immediate response was panic: every factory owner wondered who would be indicted next. Nobody denied such practices had been going on, but the main question was who had told the authorities. Who sold them out? Eventually the finger pointed to the ILGWU. The contention was that the union was upset because the violations cut into its income. After questioning, the president of Local 23–25 admitted that his office had provided records to the federal authorities. However, he said that the union would have never reported to the authorities had it not been subpoenaed by the government. It had to comply, lest it be found in contempt of court.[11] The answer was curious. Why should the union be defensive about reporting actions that violated its contract and thus hurt its members? Furthermore, if the union had records showing contractors' violations, why had it not exposed the matter earlier, rather than waiting for a federal summons?

In any event, the union's curious attitude has only emboldened contractors to ignore the contracts even more. Its attitude also discourages vigilant workers from reporting violations. Conditions in the shops have deteriorated further. The situation is so bad that more and more Chinese women have ventured uptown to work in non-Chinese-operated factories in the Seventh Avenue Garment District. Workers there belong to the same union, but to a different local, and Chinese workers have found conditions there much better than those in Chinatown. They no longer have to work from seven in the morning until seven at night, they get overtime pay, and piece rates are calculated correctly. Some women say they are much happier there, and swear never to work in Chinatown shops again. Local 23–25 is clearly not enforcing union contracts in the Chinatown shops.

However, the ILGWU still tries to shift the blame to imports. And since the union has no leverage over the manufacturers' investment decisions, its response has been to lobby in Congress for a rollback of imports to 25 percent of the U.S. market. In fact, the union has sponsored several citywide protests against imports. One can imagine how difficult it is for Chinese women to demonstrate against imports made by Chinese women in Hong Kong, Taiwan, and the People's Republic—where many have only recently come from. Lobbying Congress to pass import restrictions is an uphill battle. There is stiff opposition from many forces, including retailers who profit from markups of several hundred percent on imported items and export industries, such as the aircraft and chemical industries, that fear import retaliation from other nations. In 1986 Congress passed a resolution to protect the domestic textile industry, a close ally of the garment industry, but President Reagan vetoed the bill, claiming that a trade war with other textile-exporting countries would harm the national interest.

Underlying the union's failure to enforce contracts is the belief that enforcement would put contractors out of business. But it is not clear whether the problem is real. While Chinese contractors complain about loss of business, every day there are dozens of want ads for seamstresses in the Chinese-language papers. The contractors' complaints may simply be a ploy for forcing the union to accept lower wages for the workers. Moreover, in recent years retailers have developed a strategy of encouraging fast-changing fashions. To keep up with rapidly changing styles, they need faster deliveries and greater production volume. This growing "spot market" has led to increases in jobs for Chinatown factories. While some individual shops may not be doing well, it is not necessarily true of the industry in China-town as a whole. Incompetent contractors who use obsolete pro-duction methods create their own problems; they would not survive in any event. Recently there has been a new development: two Hong Kong garment companies have set up factories in Chinatown. They evidently believe that, even with the higher wages, they will be able to make money in New York by employing modern production methods and locating nearer to the retail markets.[12]

Ultimately, whatever problems face the industry, the union is not expected to solve them. However, that is no excuse for the union to accept the contractors' view of the situation and not enforce con-tracts. If the industry is declining, does that justify the union's failure to enforce labor standards? Why should Chinese workers be the victims of this arrangement?

WOMEN'S RIGHTS

The blatant contradictions are hard to cover up. Since their mobilization in 1982, Chinese women have been stirred up and have shown more interest in union affairs. They now expect more from their union, and certainly they are more critical of its leadership. Some women realize that unless they mobilize, the union's com-mitment to them will remain limited. Thus, a group of activists gathered soon after the summer of 1982. At first they met as members of a Chinese choral group, to avoid union attention. After a few meetings one issue became paramount—the need for a children's day-care center. Among the 20,000 members of the local, there are mothers with an estimated 1,000 preschool children. Since the women work long hours and cannot leave their children at home, they bring them to work. But factory conditions are hardly suitable: several children were severely injured when they fell into elevator shafts. The women appealed to the union for help, but the president was outraged at the suggestion, declaring that child care was not its concern. Furthermore, he argued, if the union set up a day-care center for the Chinese, all other ethnic groups in the union would want one, too. And lastly, the union had no money for such a project. Eventually, after much discussion, the union did raise enough funds and took credit for establishing a day-care center, presently accommodating seventy-five children. Its original reluctance is ironic, considering the ILGWU's proud tradition of practicing "social unionism." In the 1940s, the union built housing cooperatives for its members, set up a Workers' University, and was one of the first unions to establish welfare and retirement funds.[13]

As more rank-and-file Chinese women became involved in the day-care issue, the union leadership has had to make some concessions, because of the important role its Chinese members play in the industry and because of their impact on the union. Since 1982 it understands the potentially militant nature of the rank and file. In recent years, the union has become more involved in Chinatown's community affairs, taking positions on housing, civil rights, immigration, and even public-safety issues. However, these involvements, if continued, may push the union into community politics and ultimately shift the focus of its power from the union local to the community. This "decentralizing" development is not what the union leadership wants, and that's why at present none of its leaders is Chinese.

THE NEED TO BUILD COMMUNITY-BASED LABOR ORGANIZATIONS

The needs of today's Chinatown workers seem at odds with the nature of American unions. They need active unions that can protect them against exploitation, but militant unionism long ago declined in this country. Today the Chinese usually have flabby business unions, interested primarily in collecting dues and protecting the union bureaucracy, and not concerned with the complex problems facing workers in an ethnic community.

The Chinese need decentralized, community-oriented labor organizations to deal with their problems; this pattern is contrary to the model of American unions in the last fifty years, which stresses centralized, nationwide, big unions, able to confront big businesses.

But the labor movement may be forced to change in ways favorable to Chinese as well as other workers. The economy has undergone drastic transformations in the last decade: manufacturing industries are in decline; service industries and high-tech production are expanding. New production systems tend to require automation and decentralization, with fewer employees. There is, at the same time, a growing underground economy that requires immigrant labor and subcontracting systems. All these changes undermine the foundations of established American unions. If they are to survive, they will have to make fundamental changes. One of the most important would be to organize labor effectively in ways and places that are ignored today, including industries employing minority and immigrant workers. As we have seen, the problems of Chinatown's workers are those that the ILGWU and the Hotel and Restaurant Employees and Bartenders Union will have to confront and solve in order to survive.

GRASS-ROOTS ORGANIZING AND COALITION BUILDING

9

THE Chinese community must develop grass-roots organizations based on new political alignments cutting across traditional clan, village, trade, and tong divisions. Only then can the community confront its problems and pressure government authorities to respond to its needs. However, the first task for these organizations must be to counter the monopoly of the traditional associations.

During the period of dominance of the Chinese Consolidated Benevolent Association and the Chinese Nationalist Party, any new political force was quickly ostracized, threatened, and easily eliminated. That happened to the Chinese Hand Laundry Alliance in the 1950s. It is not surprising, therefore, that the next major organizing effort in Chinatown did not occur until the late 1960s, when the influence of the Nationalist Party declined. The grass-roots movement was led by the educated, second-generation Chinese in the community. Furthermore, their efforts paralleled a larger movement in American society that had profound effects on minority communities.

THE EVOLUTION OF
LEFT ORGANIZATIONS

A group called I Wor Kuen ("Righteous and Harmonious Fists," named after the paramilitary organization prominent during the Boxer Rebellion whose purpose was to expel Westerners from China in the late 1890s) was the first activist organization to appear in 1969. Several others soon followed. Members of these groups came from similar political backgrounds. In the late 1960s, Asian Americans on the East and West Coasts became involved in the anti-Vietnam War movement on college campuses. Influenced by the racial consciousness of the blacks, they began to see the war in Southeast Asia differently from white radicals. They saw the American invasion of Vietnam as a racist war against Asians. The most politically conscious formed their own organizations, such as the Asian American Political Alliance and the Asian Coalition, at Columbia University, Princeton, and Sarah Lawrence. They formed Third World alliances with blacks and Latino student groups, and made demands on college administrations for minority admissions and ethnic-studies programs.

Some activists, caught up in the national fervor, turned to political activities beyond the campuses. Inspired by the Black Panthers and the Young Lords, they wanted to organize in their respective communities. This is how political organizations like the I Wor Kuen, the Food Co-op, the Workers' Viewpoint, and groups of similar persuasion came into being.

A few founding members of these organizations were from Taiwan and Hong Kong, but most were second-generation Asian Americans attending elite institutions. They were proud, intelligent, politically aware, and deeply affected by the turbulent events of the time: the antiwar movement, the rebellion in urban ghettos, the assassinations of political leaders (Malcolm X, Martin Luther King, Jr., Bobby and Jack Kennedy, Black Panthers, and others), strikes on college campuses, the Palestinian struggle in the Middle East, and the student movements in France and Japan. Specifically relevant to the Asian

students were developments in the People's Republic of China during
its Cultural Revolution. Many saw China as the symbol of self-reliant
Third World people standing up to imperialism and oppression.
These highly compressed and powerful influences created the background against which the I Wor Kuen and others started their work
in Chinatown. Ideologically, they were socialist; organizationally,
they followed cadre-form party structure.

Even though the activists understood little about Chinatown, they
wanted to build a community movement as part of the worldwide
movement for social revolution. They believed that the working
people of Chinatown—who were exploited by their landlords and
employers, oppressed by the feudal institutions, and victimized by
the racist American society—would naturally rise up once their consciousness had been raised.

Ideological education in building ethnic pride was the first order
of work. Since the McCarthy era of the 1950s, no Chinatown book-
store dared to sell materials from the People's Republic of China,
and no theater dared to show its movies, for fear of retaliation from
the anti-Communist Chinatown establishment. In 1969 the I Wor
Kuen began showing PRC movies weekly in a parking lot, sold
magazines in its store, and published articles lauding the accomplishments of the People's Republic. In its organ, *Getting Together*, it
displayed the Five Star banner of the PRC and quoted the sayings
of Chairman Mao. The organization also held public celebrations on
October 1, China's National Day. These actions broke the community taboo on any public expression on PRC issues. Most importantly, the activists hoped that by showing how the people of
China struggled to take control of their own destiny, they could
inspire Chinatown's population to do the same.

"Serve the people"—a concept borrowed from the People's Republic of China—describes their strategy for reaching the people.
By providing free medical care and legal assistance, and by handling
residents' housing complaints and workers' grievances, the organizers
hoped to gain the trust of the people. However, their programs for
the people were to be different from those of the social-welfare

agencies. They were meant to educate the masses, to show that the existing political system was incapable of caring for the poor and racial minorities, and to show that basic changes could come about only through social revolution.[1]

Their militant attacks against racism and exploitation exposed problems in the community for all to see. This breath of fresh air had a stimulating effect on this previously silent ghetto. The activists successfully mobilized residents against racial discrimination. One of the first mobilizations in 1974 centered on demands that a construction company hire Chinese workers to build Confucius Plaza, a thirty-story, federally funded, low-to-middle-income housing project in Chinatown. Another mobilization in 1975 served to protest police brutality against a Chinese resident. In both cases the activists brought residents into the streets to demonstrate—something that had not happened before. Their actions revealed the political potential of the community.

However, conditions in Chinatown were far more complicated than the activists had anticipated. Residents, in most instances, could not relate to radical views or to the concept of Third World unity. Even on issues involving mass protests, the activists were not able to win the people over ideologically or to consolidate organizational strength. For example, in May of 1975, the activists mobilized 20,000 demonstrators against police brutality. Yet, a few months later, another mass demonstration was organized—this time by the Chinese Consolidated Benevolent Association against the proposed closing of the local Fifth Precinct. Once again 20,000 demonstrators came out into the streets. The two mass protests drew from the same base but were organized by different leaderships, for almost completely opposite objectives. One could conclude that the community was militant in fighting for its rights but not committed to following any group.

Failure of the activists to develop a strong following was rooted in their concept of vanguard politics. They thought of themselves as leaders and not as part of the masses. When political consciousness was not aroused on one issue, the radicals switched to another, never concentrating on a few main goals to gain and consolidate solid support. Moreover, they tended to stay away from the workers' day-to-day struggles at their workplaces.

Their organizing efforts were limited, because most activists were second-generation Chinese who could not speak Cantonese well and lacked an understanding of the Chinese approach to community politics. Without a broad base, they could not challenge the tongs, the traditional associations, and the CCBA. For example, the very first action of the I Wor Kuen in Chinatown in 1970 set the pattern of its future relationship with the tongs. The demonstration was against tourist buses in Chinatown. The IWK organized protests at the bus stop where the tourists disembarked, demanding that the bus company end its demeaning and racist tours, which brought out-of-town people to gawk at the Chinese as if they were freaks in a circus. After the demonstration a warning came from one of the tongs, suggesting that any further action would result in violent consequences. The IWK stopped the protests and recruited supporters, in and out of the community, to stand guard in front of its headquarters in anticipation of gang attacks. It was later learned that the bus company had an agreement with a tong that protected the souvenir shop to which the tourists were brought. The IWK learned that it was dangerous to interfere with the interests of the tongs.

By the mid-1970s, the activists realized they had to tone down their "revolutionary" rhetoric, and to improve their relationship with the people in the community. Workers' Viewpoint established a front organization, Asian Americans for Equality, which less political people could join. The I Wor Kuen developed the Progressive Chinatown People's Association (PCPA), a community organization of progressive workers, students, and other residents.

Both new organizations focused on issues in which they had had some success in the past, such as affirmative action and civil rights. Thus, they seemed to identify as the main contradiction in the community the one that came from outside—i.e., racial oppression. This new approach lessened confrontations within the community and made internal coalitions possible.

In the meantime, to improve their access to the community, both groups recruited more Cantonese-speaking, community-based individuals. On a number of issues, particularly housing for the poor, both the AAFE and the PCPA were tireless in their efforts.

Nevertheless, they still saw themselves as fighting *for* the people and not *with* the people. Nor had the activists resolved the contradiction between their community-service programs and their political-education programs. For example, there were many in the community with serious grievances, who exhausted all other channels and finally came to the activists for help. The activists tended to publicize these cases in order to educate the community. However, in the end, they were not always able to resolve the original problem, and some residents accused them of being opportunists.

Within the activists' organizations political conflicts developed. Those members dedicated to social-service programs were accused of promoting sham reforms. Their critics advocated the formation of a solid cadre with "highly consolidated programs, strategy and tactics" to lead the masses.[2] Political splits occurred within almost all the major groups, with violent physical confrontations taking place in the AAFE.

The Chinatown activists, like many on the American left at the time, came to the conclusion that they needed to study theory in order to get the "correct line" for their political work. They engaged in endless polemics on the correct line, based on arguments relying on highly abstract, theoretical material. During this period of internal debate, the activists became increasingly intolerant of others. Several groups folded because of internal differences. By the late 1970s, the AAFE and the PCPA were the only two remaining activist groups.

Some of the activists who dropped out of these groups joined with others to take up more specialized community work in the Chinatown Health Clinic, the Asian American Legal Defense and Education Fund, the Chinese Staff and Workers Association, and rank-and-file union work in the ILGWU. These new groups began to play important roles in the community. As a result, on a number of very important community issues, such as the organizing of the restaurant workers, the AAFE and the PCPA were relegated to peripheral roles.

The activists' lack of success in community work did not trouble them at first, because they were recognized as the vanguard of the Asian American movement. The activists worked closely with the leftist, labor, and minority groups on a variety of political projects. In fact, they had greater rapport with these outside groups, with whom they shared similar backgrounds and a common political language, than with the Chinese community.

Furthermore, they had over the years developed a reputation as the spokespersons for the progressive faction of Chinatown. As a result, they were prominent in the media and helped to counter the conservative image of Chinatown presented by the traditional associations.

However, the outside world was changing quickly. Minority movements were declining, the war in Vietnam ended, youth became less involved in social issues, and the Chinese model changed after the death of Mao.

NEW DIRECTION
OF THE LEFT

The American political climate changed dramatically with the advent of the Reagan Administration and its conservative agenda. Many leftist groups were alarmed by the resurgence of the far right. Pointing to incidents such as the Klan murder of five civil-rights demonstrators in Greensboro, North Carolina, the AAFE called for the formation of a broad coalition against fascism. This development, coinciding with the collapse of the center of the Democratic Party, created organizing opportunities for progressive rank-and-file labor and minority groups in the party. The Rainbow Coalition, built around the leadership of Jesse Jackson, met these conditions precisely. Participation in the American political system and its electoral politics became the center of AAFE activities.

The Progressive Chinatown People's Association approved of this new direction. One of its national leaders, Wilma Chan, argued in an article that "electoral work should become part of a political strategy for our communities and cities . . . . [We should] build a base of support in the areas where Asians are concentrated, and run for local office to further the struggles of our people."[3]

This new direction for the Chinatown left suggests a redefinition of its role and that of the Chinese community. The left's new stance broadened its political constituency to include all Asians as part of the coalition fighting the far right. The internal unity of Chinatown, and of all Asians, is basic, according to this formulation. The Progressive Chinatown People's Association changed its name to the Chinese Progressive Association. Dropping the word "Chinatown" and replacing it with "Chinese" is indicative of this shift of emphasis.

Both the CPA and the AAFE began to participate wholeheartedly in electoral politics during the 1984 election as part of the Rainbow Coalition. Although the two groups tend to support different political candidates, they both work to gain access to politicians. They have also had their own members run for elected office.

The activists have certain advantages in the political arena. In their previous work with the American left, they learned a great deal about politics and political jargon. Thus, they are able to communicate easily in a political environment. Also, their previous connections are useful in building alliances with liberal, reform, and minority factions in the Democratic Party at both the city and state levels. Being young, energetic, articulate, and motivated to do grass-root political organizational work, they usually impress outsiders as a future force in the Chinese community. So, while the activists have not been particularly successful within the community, they have gained a respectable reputation outside it.

Both the CPA and the AAFE have become active in the city and state's Democratic politics. They realize that the Chinese community lacks voting strength, but they are willing to compensate for it by hard work at the grass-roots level for the candidates they choose to support. Also, since they are Asians, their appearance in a candidate's campaign suggests broader support than is, in fact, the case.

The Chinese Progressive Association was active in the 1984 campaign of David Dinkins for Manhattan borough president. The Asian Americans for Equality was even more involved in the 1986 campaign of Governor Mario Cuomo[4] and the statewide activities of the Jesse Jackson presidential campaign. The two groups were instrumental in forming various support committees in Chinatown and in producing bilingual leaflets and other campaign literature. They advised candidates about the issues of concern to the Chinese community. They also helped in voter-registration drives and volunteered to be poll watchers on Election Day. So far, these efforts have paid off. After his victory Dinkins appointed two CPA leaders to the community board. The New York State Department of Social Services has since awarded the AAFE a grant of $1 million toward the construction of a shelter for the homeless.

The AAFE has become much more aggressive in pursuing its new strategy. Its members have run for various Democratic Party positions, including state committeeperson[5] and delegate to the state primary. The AAFE believes that by placing its members at the party's working levels, it can maximize its future influence and increase its political visibility.

The wisdom of participating in electoral politics is not hard to appreciate: political changes can come about much easier with institutional resources. So long as the Chinese are not involved politically, outside officials will ignore their problems.

ETHNIC SOLIDARITY AND ELECTORAL POLITICS

A number of Chinese Americans, particularly the professionals, are enthusiastic about involvement in American politics. To them, it is a matter of ethnic pride. They proudly point to the examples of Ms. March Fong Eu, the Secretary of State of California, and to S. B. Woo, the Lieutenant Governor of the state of Delaware, to show that "we can do it, too." These professionals contribute generously to Chinese American candidates, even when they don't live in their districts. The AAFE and many other groups are tapping this kind of support.

However, participation in electoral politics on an ethnic basis presents serious problems. For one thing, the Chinese don't have many enrolled voters. A large number of immigrants prefer to maintain permanent resident status rather than become naturalized citizens; therefore, they cannot vote. Moreover, few citizens register, and of those registered, few go to the polls. In the last several elections the number of registered voters in Chinatown was 3,000; the highest number that actually voted was 1,500.[6] This meager voting strength means that the Chinatown electorate has little influence on the outcome of elections.

Any Chinese who hopes to be elected by emphasizing ethnic issues and counting on Chinese votes will not get very far. March Eu and S. B. Woo did not get where they are by doing that. Delaware, for example, has an Asian population of less than a half of one percent.

Furthermore, there is no guarantee that a Chinese candidate is necessarily better for the community. In the 1985 New York City Council race, Virginia Kee became the first resident to run for the post. Yet her opponent, Miriam Friedlander, who was not Chinese, was more interested in the welfare of Chinatown residents. During the campaign, a Chinatown committee for Friedlander was formed to make sure that Kee would not use the ethnic issue to confuse the public. Peter Ng, a successful Chinatown real-estate broker with no previous political experience, also tried his hand in politics by running for the New York State Assembly. He ran as a Republican. According to all accounts, Ng is inarticulate and unfamiliar with general political issues, but he does have money. He spent twenty times more on the campaign than his opponent—and lost.

Backing candidates on the basis of their ethnicity is a game almost everybody is playing. It is a losing game. Worst of all, it leaves the power relations within the Chinese community unchanged. Those holding power in traditional organizations are not challenged. Furthermore, so-called community leaders with money and organizational backing could easily become politicians representing the community in the electoral process. During Mayor Koch's 1986 campaign for re-election, a Chinatown Koch-support committee was formed, with Uncle Seven and Eddie Chan as sponsors. It was later dissolved at the urging of Koch's staff.

Now that AAFE members are seeking elective posts, they are willing to work with all groups and have dropped their dogmatic positions. In the process of raising funds for its political campaigns, the AAFE has changed in two ways: it is turning more and more to the professional, non-Chinatown Asians for contributions and support; and it now encourages its members to enter establishment careers—in law, real estate, and on Wall Street.

In order to gain community support, the AAFE has taken very ethnocentric positions. For instance, in the summer of 1985, when the FDIC closed down the Golden Pacific Bank after detecting serious violations of banking regulations, the AAFE denounced the action as "racist." The AAFE took this position despite knowing that officials of the bank had issued uninsured certificates of deposit to unsuspecting clients.[7] Hundreds of depositors, with accounts involving $14.2 million, learned afterward that their money had been invested in private ventures which had failed. Later, the FDIC sold the bank holdings to the Hong Kong Shanghai Banking Corporation (HKSB).[8] The AAFE again denounced the action. Since the HKSB is a British-owned bank, leaders in the AAFE compared it to the "comprador bourgeoisie" taking over the interests of a "national bourgeoisie." These are polemical terms borrowed from the Chinese Communists which were used during the civil war to distinguish between "traitors" and "patriots."

So far, no Chinese American in New York has been elected to political office; those now holding posts, including CPA and AAFE members, were appointed by officials or selected by party functionaries. They were given these posts because they advocated positions favorable to the Asian American community.

For groups to build a political base around ethnic issues is valid. Indeed, there are a number of means of doing this—supporting bilingual education, stopping violence against Asians, defeating English-only ordinances, and promoting immigration-law reform, for example.

However, there are other issues that deeply divide Chinatown. There are those who want to see the area developed, and others who want to preserve the present supply of low-income housing. Therefore, electoral politics along ethnic lines will not solve the most pressing problems of Chinatown. This being the case, no one organization can claim to represent all Chinese.

THE MERGING OF
GRASS-ROOTS AND
ELECTORAL POLITICS

Yet almost every group from the traditional associations, the social-service agencies, the unions, and the activist organizations has claimed to speak *for* the Chinatown working people. The very existence of some organizations is justified by the service they provide to the community. However, very few workers are even directly involved. Thus, the results of existing programs have been less than impressive.

As we have seen, working people in Chinatown, even new immigrants, are not docile. Restaurant workers, the Staff and Workers Association, and the women garment workers have all shown their willingness to struggle for their rights. In fact, since the successful mobilization of the rank-and-file garment workers and the formation of independent restaurant unions, the working people of Chinatown have commanded respect and are courted by various political organizations. It is becoming clear that the activism of the working people is a potential source of political power in Chinatown. Realizing this, the Chinese Staff and Workers Association has successfully encouraged workers to serve on neighborhood committees and local community boards. These workers, who are hurt the most by gen-

trification, are much more effective spokespersons than professionals
or activists advocating their interests.

This direct "empowerment" approach—having workers participate in decision-making bodies and doing things for themselves—
can affect profoundly the way things are done and the way people
see themselves. As an example, we can look at the campaign against
gentrification and the role played by working people in the campaign.
Due to the encouragement of the Staff and Workers Association,
Chinatown residents joined a Lower East Side group called Reha-
bilitation in Action for the Improvement of the Neighborhood
(RAIN). RAIN undertakes homesteading with a twist—low-income
community people, through sweat equity, rebuild abandoned housing to be managed by the residents themselves. The buildings are
then converted into a land trust, where no individual holds the deed;
the title will be passed on in the future to other low-income people.
Under this program, people are actively involved at every step of
the process. The ultimate result is direct political empowerment.

This approach does not exclude workers from participating in
other political arenas. The working people in Chinatown need to
participate in electoral politics, but not necessarily along ethnic lines.
They need to form groups around specific needs and to ally themselves with groups with similar interests outside the community.
Recently, as we have seen, grass-roots organizations in Chinatown
joined with forces outside the community to support local candidates
such as Miriam Friedlander rather than a Chinese candidate. The
criterion for support was not ethnicity but the candidate's programs
for working people and the poor in Lower Manhattan. Chinatown
groups need no longer be trapped by a call for ethnic unity, as they
have been in the past under the rule of the Chinese Consolidated
Benevolent Association. Intercommunity alliances with those in the
larger society will enable them to voice their concerns more effectively.

The formation of intercommunity alliances is also taking place on
the gentrification issue. Several Chinatown groups have already joined
the Lower East Side Joint Planning Council, a coalition of the Cath-

olic Church, black and Hispanic tenants' committees, neighborhood artists, homestead groups, and community-development agencies. The Joint Planning Council has demanded that the city not auction city-owned, abandoned buildings on the Lower East Side to developers but convert them into community-owned, low-income housing.

Another potential key issue for the formation of an intercommunity alliance is the demand for federal enforcement of the minimum-wage law in Chinatown. Here again, Chinatown workers cannot rely on mobilization of support within the Chinese community, since there are powerful interests that oppose enforcement of federal labor standards. Chinese workers will have to join with Hispanic sweatshop workers in other parts of New York. Through an alliance, they can more effectively pressure federal and state authorities to take action.

If Chinese workers can gain political power through grass-roots organization and intercommunity alliances, they will be able to advance their own interests and transform Chinatown into a more democratic community. This is not an unrealistic expectation. While today most Chinatown residents are politically disenfranchised, they are not in a unique situation. Some of the Great Society programs of the 1960s, devised by politicians and implemented by bureaucrats without involvement of the people being served, have alienated different sectors of the general public. At the same time, hundreds of single-issue groups have advocated minority rights, programs for the poor, peace initiatives, environmental concerns, anti-nuclear issues, and programs of rank-and-file union democracy. Grass-roots groups in Chinatown are becoming part of a larger national movement. A new coalition is emerging, and existing political parties and forces such as organized labor will have to respond if they are to survive.

UNWELCOME
NEWCOMERS:
CHINATOWN
IN THE 1990S

10

TODAY Chinatown continues to expand as an ethnic enclave. Geographically, it has supplanted most of the old European immigrant neighborhoods on the Lower East Side, leaving a mere trace of Little Italy—the two-block area of tourist restaurants on Mulberry Street. It has become so crowded and expensive in Chinatown that many of the new immigrants who work there have been forced to the outer boroughs, where cheap housing is available. As a result, satellite Chinatowns have sprung up throughout the city in places such as Flushing, Queens, and Sunset Park, Brooklyn.

Chinatown's underground economy has undergone drastic changes since the 1980s, mainly due to the huge influx of immigrants from mainland China. Their heavy and sustained flow stems from the 1979 normalization of relations between the United States and China—whereby China was granted a yearly immigration quota of 20,000—and from Deng Xiaoping's policy of market reforms that have relaxed emigration restrictions for Chinese. Since the 1980s, Chinatown's ethnic composition has changed radically. Whereas its original founders emigrated from the eight counties along the Pearl River delta near Canton and its post-1965 residents came mostly from Hong Kong, Chinatown's newest immigrants hail from all over mainland China and Southeast Asia, making it a truly diverse community. A Vietnamese Chinese community has sprung up along the western rim of Canal Street; a large Fuzhounese community thrives on East Broadway; pockets of Chaozhounese now dot the neighborhood; and hundreds of food and souvenir vendors from Wenzhou crowd on Chinatown sidewalks and subway entrances. These are the fastest growing groups in Chinatown. Cantonese, the main dialect since the community's beginning in the 1880s, is ebbing in use, and for the first time in a hundred years, Chinatowners can get by with Mandarin, the official dialect of mainland China and Taiwan.

Since most of the new mainland immigrants are no longer from the Kwangtung province (where Canton is), few have relatives to sponsor them. Most enter the United States illegally, which has had a startling and unexpected effect on almost every aspect of life in Chinatown. As their numbers swell, the new immigrants are undercutting Chinatown's already saturated labor market, and driving its economy into a state of depression. It is now a place only for the desperate. The most significant impact of illegals, however, is not their number. They probably constitute less than 20 percent of the population, yet they have shifted the community's economic and social balance so significantly that it is impossible to understand Chinatown today without a careful study of them.

THE UNDOCUMENTED FROM FUZHOU

Most illegal Chinese have come from Malaysia and the coastal regions of mainland China. By far, the largest group is from Fuzhou, a major seaport of five million people located on the northern coast of Fujian province, across from Taiwan. The Fujian province and its adjacent neighbor, the province of Kwangtung, were the two most important sites of overseas Chinese immigration in the past centuries. Today, they also have the fastest rate of economic growth. Yet very little is known about the Fuzhounese, because they speak a dialect that has no relationship to any other, not even to the southern Fujianese Minan dialect spoken by people from Xiamen and Taiwan. They are renowned, however, for their close-knit social networks, which are reinforced by their city's geographic remoteness. For centuries, the Fuzhounese have been a seagoing people who have established large settlements all over Southeast Asia, and it was only in the early 1970s that they began to emigrate to North America and to settle in New York City. The first group were seamen who jumped ship. As undocumented immigrants, they could not legally apply to have their relatives follow them, so when border controls in China relaxed in the mid-1980s, waves of Fuzhounese began to leave illegally. But a small portion of them did become naturalized as part of the 1987 Amnesty Program and a 1989 Executive Order issued by President Bush, which permitted Chinese nationals already in the U.S. to apply for status adjustments in the aftermath of the Tiananmen Massacre. In the 1990s, the exodus of Fuzhounese has intensified, with hundreds of illegals arriving each month.

Chinatown, New York, is the illegals' main destination because of the city's numerous low-wage jobs. The community also serves as an ideal cover for the human-smuggling networks that bring them in. Illegal Chinese immigration is not new to this country. After the Chinese Exclusion Act of 1882, the only way Chinese could immigrate to the U.S. was to be smuggled in through the Canadian or Mexican borders or to declare oneself the "paper son" of a U.S. citizen. But earlier illegal migration fades in magnitude when compared to the numbers pouring in today.

Chinatown residents are wary of the Fuzhounese because they are said to be obsessed with earning money. They are the *gan-she-qui*, the "daredevils," who operate take-out restaurants in the most dangerous ghettos; they are the undocumented "snake people"—the people who wiggle their way through. The Fuzhounese have been blamed for everything that is wrong in Chinatown: barbaric competition; slave wages; unemployment; moral depravation; lawlessness; and ransom kidnapping, a crime once unknown in the neighborhood. Yet most Fuzhounese, like most Chinese immigrants, are honest people who have come to New York City in search of menial work, who believe wholeheartedly in the American Dream and in eventually saving enough money to start their own businesses. Their American experience usually begins at the intersection of East Broadway, Eldridge, Division, and Market Streets, the site of dozens of employment agencies, where at all times of the day hundreds of young males can be seen milling about, looking for work.

A typical employment agency is a one-room office, divided by a high counter and iron bars that rise up to the ceiling, a layout also found in ghetto liquor stores. On one side of the barrier, workers stand in clusters, chatting and smoking, anxiously waiting for their numbers to be called. On the other side, female clerks busily take phone calls from employers looking for workers. As the clerks jot down the details from the callers, they shout through a loudspeaker, calling out the workers' numbers, describing the positions, and dispatching the workers to the locations of the jobs. Job announcements are also posted on slips that line the walls of the agencies. They typically read: "Seeking Fuzhounese to work as take-out delivery man, $50/week, plus tips, worker must provide his own bicycle, Uptown," or "Nanny, $800/month, New Jersey," or "Fuzhounese, construction work, no skills necessary, Long Island, transportation provided, $40/day." These are all ten-hour-a-day, six-day-a-week jobs; they are temporary positions without benefits. It is a well known fact to employers that the East Broadway agencies cater to Fuzhounese undocumented workers, and a quick glance at the posted announcements shows that employers call in from all over the East Coast—New Jersey, Connecticut, Maine, and as far away as Ohio and North Carolina. Few of the ads provide the names of the cities or towns where the jobs are, but this does not concern job hunters; it matters little where they spend their "purgatory existence."

The majority of jobs are in restaurants: as deep-fry handlers in Chinatown restaurants; as cashiers in North Carolina; as dishwashers and kitchen helpers in Chicago. Some higher-wage jobs are also listed: an assistant to a sushi chef in a Japanese restaurant in Colts Neck, New Jersey; nurse's aid to a "Western" infirm senior citizen in Connecticut; housemaid in Philadelphia for a monthly salary of $1,000. All require at least some command of English.

Hiring workers is simple. Employers need only find the telephone or fax number of an employment agency in a Chinese-language newspaper and inquire about the availability of workers. The agencies expect potential employers to offer below-minimum wages, nor are employers expected to pay an agency fee, which is usually 15 percent of a worker's first-month paycheck. Rather, it is the workers who pay the agency fee, which means that a busboy offered a wage of $3 an hour actually makes $2.55 an hour. Although they violate the law, employers need not worry about the terms they offer because they know most workers have Temporary Work Status.[1]

The employment agencies target Fuzhounese precisely because they lack the papers that would protect their rights as American workers. The agencies that control the blue-collar labor market do not offer jobs to other ethnic Chinese, unless they, too, can prove they are illegal workers. In the past five years, undocumented Fuzhounese have penetrated the garment, construction, restaurant, and domestic-service trades, and many can be found in Chinese take-out restaurants in the city's ghettos and suburbs as well as in small villages in upstate New York and New England. But not all employers who hire Fuzhounese are Chinese. In fact, the kitchens of mid-priced Continental or American restaurants in Manhattan are filled with Chinese workers. Small non-Chinese-owned electronics factories in New Jersey, construction companies specializing in loft renovation in SoHo, and Long Island farms alike use Chinese employment agencies as labor contractors, and expect them to handle the selection, transport, and payment of their workers. If a construction company hires an unskilled carpenter for below-average wages, it does not want to know about the worker's legal status, nor is it interested in giving the job to anyone else.

INDENTURED SERVITUDE

Fuzhounese workers agree to work for below-minimum wages because they need to take any job that will enable them to pay off their debt to snakeheads—the smugglers who arrange for their transport to the U.S. The current cost for illegal transport from Fuzhou to the United States is approximately $30,000 to $35,000, and those who want to emigrate must raise $1,500 to cover the initial cost of the trip (a hefty sum, considering that the average yearly income in China is $400). The remaining sum is paid to a snakehead upon arrival in America. If a new immigrant is lucky, he or she can borrow from relatives in the U.S.—usually at 3 percent interest—but to pay off $30,000 in three years requires saving approximately $10,000 a year, or $800 a month, which is close to these immigrants' average monthly income.

The number of people who have come from Fuzhou recently is so great that relatives in the United States can no longer offer to help, for they are already burdened with the debts of those who immigrated earlier. New arrivals have been forced to borrow from the snakeheads at an interest of 30 percent. But a new arrival usually makes only $800 a month, which is just enough to pay the interest portion of the loan; they soon learn that it will take far more than three years to pay off the snakeheads' due.

If debts are not paid, "enforcers"—usually youth-gang members contracted by snakeheads—will resort to threats and often torture. One punishment favored by the enforcers is to hit a person under the shoulder blades with a hammer, causing an injury that does not harm the person's ability to work but is extremely painful. It is an injury meant to be remembered. Another tactic of the enforcers is to threaten the debtor's relatives with his imminent execution, and convince them to come up with cash quickly. In 1991, a hysterical man called 911 pleading for help for his kidnapped relative. The word "kidnapping" brought the FBI to the case. Upon breaking into the Brooklyn apartment where the relative was held, the FBI found a man half-dead, handcuffed to a bedpost, beaten with crowbars, and burned with cigarettes. It was this incident that first alerted American law enforcement to the brutality of human smugglers in Chinatown.

In some cases, the snakeheads simply incarcerate the undocumented. In 1992, a team of Brooklyn police discovered a human-smuggling scheme while investigating a youth-gang extortion case. When they broke into an apartment building in the Hispanic section of Sunset Park, the police found thirteen undocumented Fuzhounese who had been locked in the cellar for as long as fourteen months. Unable to pay off the snakehead's fee, these Fuzhounese immigrants had become virtual slaves to the members of the Fuching (Fujian Youth) gang. During the day, they worked at restaurants and laundries affiliated with snakeheads, and at night they were taken back to the cellar, where they were forced to hand over the money they had earned that day. Such practices are reminiscent of the Chinese indentured-labor system that existed on the West Coast during the late nineteenth century, when immigrants were under "contract" to Chinese merchant-creditors.

For obvious reasons, Fuzhounese live in constant fear of defaulting on their debts. They work six days a week in a "regular" job, and then work a seventh day, euphemistically called the "cigarette day," to earn pocket money for nonessential items such as cigarettes and candies. Most Fuzhounese also work a second job: an illegal might work a ten-hour shift as a dishwasher and follow it with a shift as a night watchman in a Chinatown office building. Most illegals are male. Because migration from China requires long-term planning, extended families send young men to the United States first, hoping the rest of the family will follow soon after. Still, wives and sisters who join their husbands or siblings come to the U.S. through the same smuggling system. They, too, are forced to borrow from the snakeheads.

Illegals live a Spartan existence, often sharing with twenty other men a 200-square-foot room jammed with double- and even triple-decker bunk beds made from flimsy two-by-fours. Landlords rent out such "bed-placements" at $90 a month. To cut down on costs, some tenants rent out their bed-placements for a portion of the day.

It is not unusual for Lower Manhattan fire departments to find dozens of families living in claustrophobic quarters in the basements of tenement buildings. There are hundreds of such illegal residences in the Chinatown area. People sleep under rusty pipes, dangling wires, and exposed asbestos, without heat, hot water, or proper kitchen and toilet facilities. And they eat *man tou*, steamed buns from northern China, which sell ten for a dollar—enough for two days' sustenance—to pay back the snakehead's fee.

Although their life is hard, few illegals would admit leaving China was a mistake. Once they are here, after so much suffering, many feel it is pointless to complain. Mr. and Mrs. Lin arrived in New York three years ago after surviving a horrifying forty-five-day trip across the Pacific on a 100-foot unseaworthy fishing boat. The only work Mr. Lin could find was in a New Haven restaurant, where he labored twelve hours a day and slept on the kitchen floor at night. Mrs. Lin's situation was just as difficult; she lived in a one-room apartment in Chinatown with her in-laws and put in a fourteen-hour day as a seamstress at home. Mrs. Lin said she often tried to work more, but her in-laws complained about the noise at night. After three years in the U.S., the Lins have paid off only half their debt. Not surprisingly, Mrs. Lin has tried to dissuade her relatives back home from coming to the U.S., but she knows her pleas fall on deaf ears. "They think I am coldhearted and unwilling to help," she said and explained that in China tales of American hardship are often interpreted as "socialist propaganda" or as betrayal by uncaring relatives. Chinese continue to believe what the snakeheads tell them: that everyone in America can earn $30,000 in three years, a promise that convinces many would-be immigrants that any hardship can be endured.

WHY DO THEY COME?

All is not well in China. Ever since the free-market reforms of the late seventies, China's economy has undergone tremendous dislocations. Deng's famous policy—"Those able to get rich should get rich first, and others will follow"—has brought rapid economic expansion and heightened people's material expectations. In the summer of 1994, when I visited the relatives of *Golden Venture*[2] inmates in China, I realized that illegals are usually from well-off families. In fact, many of them made their money during the initial liberalization period. Since 1978, privatization has brought great economic opportunity and unchecked competition, creating an environment in which only the young, ambitious, and ruthless prosper. The new elite has also transformed Chinese politics, for they are often complicit in bribing the party officials who monopolize the most lucrative enterprises. To get ahead in China's corrupt economy, the average Chinese citizen must constantly pay off officials—a much resented practice. It is not surprising, then, that illegals, while admitting their exodus is largely due to economic factors, insist they leave for political reasons as well. They consider themselves dissenters in an unscrupulous Communist regime, and are also not averse to using China's "one-child policy" as a reason for seeking political asylum.

Today, China's economic growth is concentrated in the southern coastal areas near Hong Kong and Taiwan, where an export-oriented economy is thriving, financed by foreign investment. With communes disbanded, land, produce, and equipment are no longer owned collectively. Across the country, goods and services must be purchased in cash, forcing people from interior and remote rural areas where the economy is stagnant to migrate to southern coastal cities in search of cash jobs. But the newly emerging industries have not grown large enough to accommodate this enormous demand for work. Cities such as Canton or Fuzhou are inundated with "out-of-province people," who loiter in street corners, bus stops, and train stations, waiting for jobs as day laborers. According to Chinese government statistics, there are currently 130 million people roaming the country in search of work. This floating population includes children, who live on the streets, are ill-fed and poorly clothed, a presence that reminds many of the human deprivation of pre-1949 China. There is no doubt that migration from rural or urban regions, from north to south, has brought unchecked inflation, congestion, depressed wages, high unemployment, and social disorder to Chinese cities in an infant stage of industrial development.

In China's unregulated labor market, factory owners—both foreign and domestic—prefer rural workers because they "are less demanding and work harder." For example, the highly profitable Reebok shoe factory in Fuzhou, which is housed in a massive complex in the free-enterprise zone, attracts few city workers precisely because its wages are low and its hours long. Rural workers cannot lobby for better conditions, since labor organizing is prohibited in China. In fact, the first group to be rounded up after the June 4th Massacre in 1989 were labor leaders.

Chinese are not only emigrating to America. The undocumented have been smuggled into Taiwan, Japan, Korea, Hong Kong, Australia, and even Europe. In 1995, the Czech government broke up a Chinese smuggling ring when Prague authorities became aware of a Chinese restaurant that employed more than eight hundred people but could fit only eight tables in its tiny dining room. Chinese are also leaving for other Asian countries. One young female taxi driver from Fuzhou attempted to enter Japan at Narita Airport three times with a phony passport, but was turned back each time, at great financial cost. She then tried to smuggle herself into the U.S. in a trunk stored under the deck of a cargo ship, only to be discovered and returned after four days at sea. Undaunted, she is now trying again. "If you want to make something of yourself," she explained, "even if all you want is to find a good husband, you've got to get out."

CHINATOWN'S SLAVE MARKET

Because the federal census does not offer reliable data on the undocumented, there is no accurate estimate of New York's Fuzhounese population. Some officials give a figure of 150,000, although law-enforcement officials tend to exaggerate that number in order to lobby for more funds for their agencies. One reason the Fuzhounese population is difficult to count is that they are highly mobile and do not all live and work in Chinatown. What is certain, however, is that their presence has caused wages to drop significantly. Chinatown wage earnings were already low by American standards before the influx of illegals. For years, garment ladies, although members of the International Ladies Garment Workers Union, did not earn union-rate wages, making four dollars an hour, three dollars less than the union minimum wage. In the last few years, conditions have steadily declined, and today garment seamstresses complain that wages are as low as two dollars an hour.

Even though working conditions are terrible, Chinese with proper work documents realize they are lucky to find any work at all. A few years ago, most seamstresses could count on working ten months a year. Now, most of them work only a few days a week, and make less than $200 a month. In the restaurant business, the situation is the same. A local Chinese newspaper quotes a worker as saying: "Dishwashing jobs used to pay $800 a month. Then the 'Amigos' [Mexicans] came, willing to work for $750. Now we must compete with the Fuzhounese, who will work for $500 a month." Old Chinatown residents resent the illegals who will work for any wage under terrible conditions. Some Fuzhounese even take work home in violation of New York's labor law, and now one finds Fuzhounese men working as clothing sewers, once the exclusive domain of women.

As jobs are more difficult to come by and as the pressure to pay off debts continues unabated, more and more illegals have fallen into a life of crime. Some become enforcers, runners, or collectors for snakeheads. Others form their own gangs and prey upon fellow illegals or resort to extortion, blackmail, or kidnapping to earn money from Fuzhounese businessmen. Gangs have been known to kidnap other snakeheads' clients at JFK Airport, force Fuzhounese women who are unable to pay their debts to work in massage parlors, and perpetrate unspeakable acts of violence. In 1994, eight Fuzhounese gangsters were arrested for kidnapping and torture. The gang chained their captives to an apartment ceiling, pulled out their nails, and burned their backs with hot iron rods. In 1993, fifteen of the Fifth Precinct's twenty-one homicide victims were Fuzhounese. In Brooklyn, in a span of three months in early 1994, the Asian crime unit arrested twenty-five Fuzhounese for violent home robberies. During the same period in Queens, forty Fuzhounese gangsters awaited trial on various murder, kidnapping, extortion, and robbery charges. And recent victims of kidnapping are no longer just Fuzhounese adults. In several recent cases, Chinatown children were kidnapped and their parents were asked to pay a few thousand dollars in ransom. Today, Fuzhounese criminals have established a reign of terror in Chinatown. The old residents who remember quieter, more peaceful days live in constant fear for their livelihood and personal safety.

INEFFECTIVE ENFORCEMENT AGAINST HUMAN SMUGGLING

In China, as in other developing countries, the initial period of modernization has created severe social and economic problems, generating enormous pressure on its citizens to emigrate. If we use Taiwan or Korea as a model, this critical period could last as long as two decades, but considering China's size and population, illegal migration may continue to be a major problem for the United States for years to come. The fact that most Chinese illegals are indentured, unlike Taiwanese or Korean migrants, makes their immigration even more complicated. And the profitability of human smuggling is driving up the numbers of illegals. Presently, the most developed smuggling network is between Fuzhou and New York, but in China's freewheeling economy other networks are developing and dozens of others may form. It is generally acknowledged that smugglers from Fuzhou travel from village to village along China's coast to recruit willing clients; thus, the scale of the smuggling networks will soon determine the momentum of this migration drive.

Although politicians and policymakers constantly debate whether illegal immigration should be further controlled or whether the undocumented are beneficial to the American economy, the real issue is that human smuggling and indentured servitude must stop. Unfortunately, American law enforcement is incapable of penetrating the smuggling networks. Chinese human smuggling has become an elaborate and sophisticated international system. Once illegals cross the U.S. border, they are under the control of enforcers. New York gangs such as the White Tigers, the Fu-ching, the Tong An, the Flying Dragons, and the Green Dragons are paid to do the snakeheads' dirty work, but they are not knowledgeable about their affairs. Local U.S. law enforcement may have cause to arrest gang members, but doing so will not affect the smugglers' operation.

The smuggling network is said to be financed and masterminded by Chinese crime bosses in Taiwan. Their operation can best be described as a global baseball game in which immigrants are transferred from Fuzhou or Wenzhou to international waters, where they are picked up by Taiwanese cargo ships or seagoing fishing boats. Once the ships are fully loaded—an important requirement, since the shipping companies are paid per head—they sail south to Thailand for refueling, cross the Pacific, and land on the coast of either Central America or Mexico. Once ashore, the smuggling crew crosses the U.S. border by land. If the ship lands in Central America, then its passengers travel through Mexico City, cross the Texan border, and head for Houston. If it lands off the Baja peninsula, then immigrants cross the border into San Diego and rest in safe houses in Monterey Park before flying to New York. This southern sea route is the best for smugglers to avoid detection by American satellite reconnaissance. The route followed by the *Golden Venture* —landing directly on the American shore—is the most risky.

Of course, the most comfortable way to travel to the U.S. is by plane. The trick is to find an airport where ground security is so lax or, better, so corrupt that Chinese with questionable identification papers will not be detained. This may require traveling to Budapest or to Moscow before attempting to board a U.S.-bound plane. Every immigrant's hope is to travel undetected; if detected, however, most seek political asylum. Traveling by air to the U.S. is much chancier than by sea. Since it is not as profitable, the snakeheads do not recommend air travel. Plane tickets are expensive, and the size of planes limits the number of people who can be smuggled per trip. The Immigration and Naturalization Service rarely apprehends illegals at U.S. borders or airports. Even when they do, INS officials almost never have the time or the facilities to prosecute illegals on the spot. Once bonds are posted, illegals are usually released pending deportation hearings. (The passengers aboard the *Golden Venture* were imprisoned because their dramatic arrival and great number embarrassed the INS, which had to act forcefully to maintain its image.)

The Chinese government claims to have passed strict capital-punishment laws to deter human smuggling. During my visit to Fuzhou, however, I saw few signs of restriction. Pretending to help a friend get to the United States, I had no difficulty finding snake-heads. While hanging around a café and later a candy store one afternoon, I met four lower-ranking snakeheads who spend their days circling Fuzhou, competing for customers. Each promised a better deal: U.S. entry by plane; a money-back guarantee; a fifty-fifty split for the cost of bail and lawyers' fees if caught. The Chinese government has not created incentives to limit smuggling. In fact, the government has long considered overseas Chinese a national asset, believing that the more people emigrate, the lower unemployment will be and the higher foreign-exchange reserves will grow from remittances. Government departments have organized "official" cultural, trade, and business delegations to foreign countries, which give officials and their relatives the opportunity to leave the country permanently. On one visit to China, I came across a government agency whose main purpose was to provide technical workers temporary employment in foreign countries. Deputies of that agency sold work visas, supposedly approved by foreign governments, to Chinese citizens at black-market prices, but when the immigrants arrived in their new countries they found themselves under the control of enforcers who made certain they honored their "transportation fee." In this way, the Chinese government is actually assisting and profiting from human smuggling.

ALTHOUGH American law-enforcement officials may recognize an increase in human smuggling, they are reluctant to crack down on undocumented immigrants. A federal-level law-enforcement official confided, "Most of the top brass are Italians or Irish who have an immigrant tradition of their own. Stopping people who want to come to this country for better opportunities is not their cup of tea." Even if local police discover a human-smuggling operation, they have no jurisdiction over the case, unless it involves murder, torture, kidnapping, forced prostitution, or drug trafficking. The only agency authorized to prevent human smuggling is the Immigration and Naturalization Service, but the INS lacks the resources and is too overwhelmed with other federal issues to crack down on human smuggling, an effort that would require more manpower and complex inter-agency cooperation. According to one local enforcement official, the INS is committed to preventing Chinese illegal immigration only as far as avoiding embarrassing incidents such as *Golden Venture* is concerned. U.S. authorities' lax attitude is well known in China. Once in the U.S., Chinese illegals are relatively certain they can work without harassment, arrests, or deportations by authorities, unlike illegal Chinese in Japan, Australia, or France. That's why smugglers charge the highest fee for those coming to this country. Even though most Chinese prefer Japan, because it is possible to save over $2,000 a month on a strictly enforced forty-hour week whereas in the U.S. the earnings are less under unregulated harsh labor conditions.

UNCHECKED EXPLOITATION

Undocumented workers are a bonanza for employers. Home work, thought to have disappeared in the United States fifty years ago, is a common phenomenon in Chinatown. It is also common for children under eighteen to work long hours after school and for employers to withhold wages at both unionized and non-unionized Chinese garment factories. Seamstresses tell each other: "If your wages have never been withheld, you are quite lucky. Withholding wages is considered 'normal' accounting practice these days."

In 1994, the owners of the Silver Palace restaurant, one of the largest restaurants in Chinatown, which was unionized in 1980, fired all unionized workers, claiming that wages were too high. The owners saw that it made no sense to pay union wages when there was such a large supply of cheap labor available. The workers picketed the restaurant and after more than seven months they finally won their jobs back. Meanwhile, their leader mused: "If the owners had won this one, employers all over Chinatown could have imposed any kind of conditions they wanted on working people, whether legal or undocumented. We would have become slaves." The Silver Palace restaurant incident shows that the high influx of illegals has set off a class struggle within Chinatown and that employers are using the illegals as an excuse to depress the wages of *all workers*— as a club to beat down labor opposition during this period of anti-labor sentiment.

The United States is already addicted to undocumented labor, without which its agricultural and garment industries could not survive. For some time now, American businesses have emphasized growth through deregulation and increased labor productivity. Cutting labor costs is the primary focus of American businesses, which have realized that the most effective way to downsize is by employing non-unionized labor. Immigrant labor is even more cost-efficient, because immigrants are not unionized and because they have less legal protection. Following this logic, then, the undocumented are proving to be the best labor in America's current business climate: entirely unregulated, unprotected, and highly productive. Average Americans show few moral qualms about employing the undocumented. Whenever a candidate or a nominee for public office is found to have hired undocumented domestic help, he or she chalks it up to a mental lapse on a legal technicality. Governor Pete Wilson of California, the most ardent advocate of cracking down on illegals and the initiator of the infamous Proposition 187[3] was found to have hired an illegal immigrant as domestic help in the late 1970s. Yet he emerged from public scrutiny relatively unscathed, shifting the blame for the hiring to his spouse. Even the media seem unable to understand the real issue here: that these public figures, who often earn high incomes, employ undocumented workers at minimum wage or below to save a few dollars. They violate American labor laws and most certainly exploit unprotected individuals, all to the detriment of American workers. Yet they justify their actions by claiming that American workers are not interested in these kinds of jobs anyway.

Free-market advocates condone unregulated labor with the understanding that giving jobs to the undocumented may have a disciplinary effect on American workers. In order to keep their jobs, Americans will need to work as hard and accept wages as low as the illegals do. The conservatives, on the other hand, use immigrants' willingness to work hard without benefits or government assistance as a justification to cut off all social services. The undocumented are also being used to rebut African Americans' demands to maintain affirmative-action programs.

In the aftermath of the *Golden Venture* incident, much has been learned about the tragic conditions of the Fuzhounese; however, little has been done to eliminate these abuses or to prevent American employers from exploiting the Fuzhounese. Rather, restrictive regulations have been passed against them. Scapegoating immigrants in times of economic hardship is a regular occurrence in American history. Politicians have been known to invoke images of "yellow peril" to show their tough stand on illegal immigrants but, increasingly, these attacks are aimed at immigrants of any ethnic origin other than European. In 1995, the Congress even proposed laws that would restrict benefits to legal immigrants with permanent-resident status, and since the majority of legal immigrants today are of Asian or Latino descent, these anti-immigrant bills have strong racial overtones. American outrage against exploitation of Chinese is tempered by a general view of illegals as "them," as "aliens." The implicit message is that whatever hardship Asians suffer is their own fault; emigration patterns have nothing to do with American policies. Besides, people often reason, Asians have a different value system and a peculiar tolerance for hardship.

The Chinatown political and economic establishment likes to reinforce the image that Chinese are different. They claim that Chinese are willing to work harder and expect less. When workers picketed the Jing Fong Restaurant in 1995 to protest the management's confiscation of 40 percent of the waiters' tips, the owners did not bother to deny that they were violating labor laws. They claimed that American labor standards were not applicable to Chinatown because of the intense competition and low profit margins in Chinese businesses. They also claimed that Chinese have a strong sense of ethnic solidarity and do not mind hard work if it is for other Chinese.

This view of the Chinese work ethic has many proponents. Sociologist Min Zhou in her book *Chinatown: The Socioeconomic Potential of an Urban Enclave* argues that Chinese ethnic social relations regulate economic behavior to the mutual benefit of all, for, "in Chinatown, the economic behavior is not purely self-interested, nor is it based on strict calculation in dollars." Min Zhou defends sweatshops and low wages by asserting that Chinese do not see themselves as exploited, because "the work ethic of immigrant Chinese is built on a value standard from Chinese culture and not on the one from the dominant culture."[4]

Zhou's advocacy of distinct Chinese values should please many employers. What are these Chinese values? Zhou declares that "substandard wages, which are much higher than wages in China . . . are regarded as better than no wages at all." Yet, since China's market reforms of the 1980s, the state has eliminated most labor laws and protection. In the free-enterprise zones, workers are locked in compounds, sleep and eat virtually on the factory floor, and labor fourteen hours for a wage of two dollars a day, about twenty cents an hour.

In view of China's work conditions, Chinatown's are vastly better, yet they still have no place in present-day America.

Chinese workers were invited to speak about their work environment at a town hall meeting on June 29, 1994, at P.S. 124 in Chinatown, which was attended by administrators from federal and state labor departments and representatives from the offices of members of Congress and the New York City Council. Some three hundred Chinatown residents, jammed in the elementary-school auditorium, also listened to the emotional testimonies of dozens of workers, who recited a litany of abuses at their workplaces. Government representatives learned that a twelve-hour-plus workday was common, that wages had dropped for many to only two dollars an hour, and that owners often employed members of youth gangs to threaten workers. The most consistent complaint was non-payment of wages. Surprisingly, government representatives saw these problems only in legal terms. One labor official insisted that owners' failure to pay minimum wage constituted a violation of the law and that such owners should be reported to the authorities. Another state official lectured workers that they must press for "official charges" before her office could take action against owners. The workers gasped in amazement, realizing how out of touch the authorities were with the realities of Chinatown.

Blaming the Chinese for lack of initiative is a common tactic used by officials to shrug off responsibility for conditions in Chinatown. It confirms the image of Chinese as timid and afraid of challenging the authorities. Some Asians even promote another, perhaps more positive, version of this stereotype by invoking Confucian discipline and loyalty. In the summer of 1995, *New York Times* reporter Jane Lii argued that Chinese workers enjoy working long hours for low wages and quoted one Chinese as saying: "I work hard because I am Chinese." Lii claims that Chinese would shun "westernized unions" in favor of a more familiar and paternalistic management style. In another article, she asserted that "bosses are often viewed as father figures who watch out for workers and solve their problems." When commenting on the prevalence of child labor in garment factories, Lii argued that workers often consider their employers good bosses because they are willing to violate labor laws to allow their children to work by their side.[5]

CHINATOWN LABOR MOVEMENT CONTINUES

Lii is wrong. Chinese workers are not docile. Against all odds, Chinatown labor struggles have never faltered. In 1988, the China-town Planning Council (CPC) received a federal grant to institute a training program to place workers in the construction industry. The program promised job placement after graduation. Some forty Chinese immigrants enrolled, but it soon became clear that the CPC had no program; instead, it used its trainees as menial laborers in renovating CPC's own office space, paying them five dollars an hour, half the amount stipulated by the government contract. CPC administrators expelled those who complained but the remaining trainees soon formed a union as a way to protect themselves against CPC's arbitrary policies. They, too, were promptly dismissed from the program. The trainees then decided to sue, and after considerable deliberation, the Department of Labor ruled in their favor. The CPC was told to pay back wages plus underpayment, the difference between the wages and the market rate for construction work, which was approximately $17 an hour. The total amount the CPC owed the workers came close to two million dollars. The CPC appealed but lost. It then pleaded poverty as a non-profit service organization and could not pay. It also tried to shift responsibility to the City of New York, which had contracted the CPC to run the program. The city, too, desisted, and the case dragged on.

Public-funded training programs, such as the one advertised by CPC, are greatly needed and much appreciated by Chinese immigrants, who have long been trapped in ethnic ghettos and limited to employment in the restaurant and garment trades. The opportunity to break into a new trade, such as construction, is rare for

Chinese Americans. A number of Chinese from Hong Kong in the
CPC training program had once held jobs as construction workers,
but they were unable to find such jobs in the U.S. because of the
restrictive nature of the construction unions, particularly toward minorities. With the CPC case, it became clear that neither the federal
nor the city government had any intention of integrating the construction trade. But the CPC trainees did not give up. They decided
to make a two-pronged attack on the construction industry. First,
they sought to expose the CPC, picketing its annual fund-raising
events and dropping leaflets at the homes of its board of directors.
(And after six years the city and the CPC finally came up with the
funds to settle the case.) Second, the trainees formed the Chinese
Construction Workers' Association, in alliance with the city-wide
Coalition to End Racism in the Construction Trade. Chinese workers
began to fight for jobs at construction sites alongside African American and Latino workers. Their first real opportunity came in 1992,
when major construction of an annex to the Federal Plaza and an
extension of the Federal Court House began at Foley Square, on
the edge of Chinatown. The CCWA first approached New York
City's Buildings Trade Council for consideration, but the council
refused. The CCWA then mobilized the Chinatown community in
two major demonstrations in which close to a thousand residents
participated. Demonstrators held banners that read "Stop Exclusion"
and "Equal Access to Jobs," and hundreds of garment seamstresses
took time off from work to show their support for Chinatown construction workers. One seamstress explained: "I don't know any
English, nor do I have any skills; that's why I am slaving away in a
garment factory. But it is wrong for the Americans to exclude Chinese
who have construction skills from getting jobs." After negotiating
with the Chinese Construction Workers' Association, the contractors
at Foley Square finally agreed to hire a hundred Asians. It was a
victory for Chinese immigrants whose attempts to integrate into the
American labor system had so often been stymied.

IN 1994, waiters and waitresses at the Silver Palace restaurant
fought to renew the union contracts they had won in 1980. Picketing

workers braved a harsh winter and a beastly-hot summer. While local residents stood by and admired their determination, few thought the restaurant workers' demands would be met, considering labor's increasing powerlessness in the U.S. and particularly in Chinatown. The restaurant waged a fierce public-relations campaign in news-papers and on the radio against the workers and even offered half-price meals to customers, yet it suffered a 70 percent loss in business. Seven months later it decided to settle with the union. This was an amazing victory for organized labor; it proved that small immigrant groups can stand at the vanguard of today's labor struggles and that their inclusion and mobilization are critical to building a new Amer-ican labor movement.

I N 1995, the Jing Fong Restaurant struggle moved China-town's labor battle to another level. The dispute began when Gang Deng, a waiter, challenged his boss for docking his tips and was fired. At the time Jing Fong management paid waiters less than a dollar an hour, without compensation for overtime—both violations of minimum-wage laws—and violated yet another law by deducting 40 percent from waiters' tips. Deng went to the Chinese Staff and Workers' Association for support. The CSWA took on the case even though no other workers from the restaurant came forward with Deng; it understood that the restaurant's management had intimi-dated the others. Several workers were even coerced to stage coun-terprotests. The CSWA helped Deng file a suit against the restaurant, and organized a picket of Chinese workers from other restaurants, union sympathizers, and student activists to get Deng rehired.

The Jing Fong management immediately understood what CSWA's actions might spawn, and set about organizing all restaurant owners in its defense. In April 1995, more than a thousand Chinese businessmen gathered at Jing Fong for a fund-raising dinner hosted by the Chinatown Restaurant Owners' Association, an unprece-dented show of unity among Chinatown restaurateurs. Bitter attacks were launched against Wing Lam, the advisor of the CSWA; he was accused of extortion and theft and labeled a "monster," a "blood-sucker," and "public enemy number one." Jing Fong hung two bright red twenty-five-foot banners which read: "Oppose the labor tyrant stirring up trouble"; the crowd chanted *"Da Dao Wing Lam,"* meaning "Beat Wing Lam Down."

Since this meeting, Lam and his family have received many threats, the seriousness of which cannot be underestimated, for the leaders of the Restaurant Owners' Association are also the leaders of Chinatown's organized-crime networks. Yai Chi Chan, president of the Restaurant Owners' Association, is also the Grand National President of On Leung tong, identified recently by federal authorities as one of the three tongs on the forefront of illegal business in Chinatown. Wing Yeung Chan, co-owner of Jing Fong, is also a leader of On Leung tong. Chan allegedly is the *dai lo*—the elder brother —of one of the most violent Chinatown groups, the Ghost Shadows. In a federal case he was indicted for murder, robbery, extortion, and illegal gambling. Chung-Ko Cheng, another of the six owners of Jing Fong who accused the Workers' Association of trying to destroy the restaurant industry in Chinatown, is a former president of the Fukien-American Association, a tong that the police believe has ties to Fu-ching youth gang—the chief enforcers of Fuzhounese illegals.[6] This coalition of restaurant owners, tong leaders, and human smugglers represents a powerful force and has the potential of creating an even more unstable atmosphere in Chinatown.

THE WOMEN'S COMMITTEE

In recent years, it has been the garment seamstresses who have won the most impressive battles in Chinatown's labor struggle. The mobilization of female Chinese immigrant workers has been fraught with difficulties, however, as the garment industry's International Ladies Garment Workers Union (ILGWU) is highly ineffective. Since the summer of 1982, when thousands of female workers demonstrated in Chinatown, demanding that employers renew their ILGWU contract, the union has not attempted to maintain the activism of Chinese workers, nor has it attempted to enforce contracts or to organize the thousands of new immigrants employed in non-union shops around the city. The ILGWU is what a Chinese person would describe as "sitting on the pot and not doing it"; i.e., permissive of all kinds of violations and abuses.

The union's decline is the result of an outdated strategy of organizing from above, a method that worked when the manufacturing industry was concentrated and when a stable labor supply existed in New York City. Since the emergence of a global economy, however, manufacturers have decentralized operations, subcontract to smaller businesses, and have begun exporting production overseas to cut down on labor costs. Without the manufacturers' cooperation, the union has lost its power over contractors. The ILGWU's survival is thus tied to an industry whose structure it can no longer control. In the 1990s, its sole interest is to continue to collect membership dues.

ILGWU's programs are limited to "Buy American," in which its members rally to persuade Congress to pass restrictive import legislation. This is hardly the most pressing issue for workers, not to mention its being highly ironic, considering that Chinese union members are asked to picket against their fellow workers in China and Hong Kong, where hourly wages are around $3.50—comparable to sweatshop wages in the U.S. By all accounts, Hong Kong has better health care, public housing, and public transportation systems than the U.S., and stricter government regulations vis-à-vis factory conditions. Even the sewing machines in Hong Kong are more modern than the ones used in the U.S.

In the United States' institutionalized labor movement, workers' rights are protected by labor bureaucrats and union officials. Workers are no longer advocates for their working conditions, as they once were. It is this scenario that has caused workers to feel dehumanized, alienated, and isolated, and which has limited their ability to fight for their rights. The only way to turn this situation around is for workers to build grassroots workers' organizations *from the bottom up*, which is precisely what the Chinese Staff and Workers' Association and its Women's Committee are attempting to do. Originally, the CSWA assisted only male restaurant workers, but it soon became clear that their wives, who usually worked in the garment industry, were also being discriminated against. In 1982, the CSWA succeeded in pressuring ILGWU to set up a day-care center, and soon after, it established a Women's Committee to focus on garment workers' needs.

The CSWA and its Women's Committee are not social-service agencies. Representatives of the CSWA and the Women's Committee share their expertise and their experiences with workers, but insist that workers plan, mobilize, and carry out their own struggle. The number of paid employees at the CSWA is kept intentionally small so that, as one staff member explains, "the workers do not think that the CSWA will do everything for them. If that were the case, we would not be able to release the full energy of the workers." This is, of course, easier said than done. It is difficult for workers to learn to do things for themselves. It is especially difficult to mobilize female Chinese workers. Rodha, a women's labor organizer, explains that "the first and most difficult task of working with Chinese women is to raise their level of self-confidence. They tend not to believe that they can accomplish things themselves, or that what they do will make a difference." Growing up in a male-dominated culture, most immigrant Chinese women are reticent and subordinate themselves to men. Once in the U.S., they feel even more vulnerable—ill at ease in English, burdened with child care, housework, and the stressful, tedious jobs they must take at garment factories to supplement the family income—which makes them feel physically and psychologically tied down and incapable of doing anything independently.

But the working conditions in garment factories have deteriorated to such an extent that female workers have come to realize they must do something. Astoundingly, they are not demanding above-minimum wages, a forty-hour work week, overtime pay, a clean working environment, or job security; they are only asking to be paid on time. It is around this demand that the women's movement has galvanized. The workers at Wai Chang garment factory took the lead. In 1990, the factory owners stopped making weekly payments to their workers, first claiming a minor cash-flow problem, and later alleging that the manufacturers had failed to pay them, even though everyone knew finished goods had been delivered and the factory had accepted new orders from the same manufacturers. Then the owners maintained they could not pay salaries because their partners had full control of the budget. As workers' demands for their wages grew more insistent, the owners threatened to report the workers to the INS and even invoked the names of Chinatown underworld figures as a means of intimidation. Six months later, the owners of Wai Chang owed one female worker $3,000, another $6,000 for a year's back pay, a couple a total of $10,000, and a seventy-year-old male worker $1,900.

In 1991, female workers from Wai Chang approached the Chinese Staff and Workers' Association for assistance. The Women's Committee helped them file a complaint with the New York State Labor Department, whose investigation quickly was halted when Department officials "could not locate the owners." The Department also refused the workers' request to contact manufacturers to withhold payment to Wai Chang until the back wages to the workers were paid. The Department claimed it could not do that, for lack of sufficient evidence against Wai Chang. The workers then filed criminal charges with the New York State Attorney General's Office, and four months later the owners, Wai Chee Tong and Stanley Chang, were charged with forty-one misdemeanor counts for failing to pay wages and failing to keep accurate payroll records. The settlement stipulated that Tong and Chang pay over $80,000 in owed wages —the largest suit ever won in the garment industry. But the prosecution could not move forward, because the two owners again "disappeared." Wai Chang workers applied for a warrant for their arrest, and spent weeks assisting the Attorney General's office in their search for Tong and Chang. Finally, on December 17, 1991, they found Stanley Chang and had him arrested. He was convicted and imprisoned for nine months, but he still claimed bankruptcy and, in the end, the workers never collected a penny. Nevertheless, Wai Chang workers' action served as an inspiration to others; the workers showed that they were not afraid to fight their bosses, even though many of them were undocumented. Theirs was a major psychological victory and a turning point in Chinese women's activism.

Soon after hearing of Stanley Chang's arrest, workers at Judy's Place Fashion, a unionized shop in Chinatown, went to the CSWA for help. The owner of Judy's Place Fashion owed them over $20,000, and the CSWA urged the New York State Labor Department and ILGWU Local 23-25 to investigate. Both started their investigations slowly, and failed to follow up when they "could not find the owner." Workers quickly realized they had to rely on their own efforts. Several took time off from their jobs to follow Jimmy Tse from his home to the other garment factory he managed in Queens. Tse fled, and workers called a press conference to alert the media, the ILGWU, and the Department of Labor to the need to take immediate action. The workers then increased pressure on Tse by holding public rallies and setting up tables in Chinatown to solicit residents' signatures. After five months, Jimmy Tse finally paid the workers of Judy's Place Fashion.

As the movement for back wages spreads, the Women's Committee has begun to recruit veterans of past struggles to explain the issues and the reasons for their battles against various factories. Today, the committee's work has expanded. Its legislative task force is working with the Center for Immigrant Rights and the Asian American Legal Defense and Education Fund to lobby New York State legislators to make withholding wages a felony. Another task force of the committee is trying to convince manufacturers not to award contracts to those who withhold wages, a campaign which has been successful with manufacturers such as Ann Taylor and CET Fashion and which has gotten support from a number of women's organizations, including the Organization of Asian Women.

In the meantime, the committee has launched educational training programs. Chinatown garment workers now meet every Sunday afternoon to discuss various issues concerning the garment industry, to plan strategies for back-wage campaigns, and even to exchange information about which employers are most difficult. In the summer of 1995, the Women's Committee expanded its efforts to Sunset

Park, Brooklyn, where many sweatshops have moved. Female activists have also persuaded their friends and relatives to participate in the Women's Committee, and the children of some of the activists have formed a youth group, which has started its own periodical, *Moving Forward*, and which holds a video workshop that documents their parents' struggles. The workshop's first production, *Organizing for Justice Against Silver Palace*, won the U.S.A. Hometown Video Festival's Best Documentary Award. The power of organized Chinese women immigrant workers has come alive over the past few years. Although one can hardly expect a few hundred immigrant women to correct the ills of the entire garment industry, something certainly can be learned from the experiences of the CSWA's Women's Committee in its successful grassroots mobilization.

As employers use all available means to cut costs and to push Chinatown workers to the verge of poverty, a new phenomenon is in the making: workers' resistance, joined even by illegals. This resistance is chipping away at the veneer of Chinatown's ethnic solidarity and giving rise to new unions and community organizations. At the same time such a split in the Chinese community is in concert with the larger class polarization taking shape in American society under the sway of a new ideology that is neo-conservative, pro-business, and in favor of limited government.

Conclusion

Before the civil-rights movement of the 1960s, the concentration of Chinese in ethnic ghettos was the result of racial segregation. Ever since, the revival of Chinatowns in the United States has been the result of greater employment opportunities for Chinese immigrants in these communities. Although some Chinese insist that they prefer living in Chinatown because they feel more comfortable among other Chinese, this sentiment merely reflects that discrimination and lack of jobs elsewhere make them feel uncomfortable and bound to the Chinese community. In fact, the preference to live in Chinatown is hardly cultural. Chinatown, after all, has always been a ghetto plagued by poverty, crowded housing, unsanitary conditions, and crime, and deficient in American legal protection and the rule of law. Few Chinese would spend their lives there if they could help it, yet the American public continues to believe that Chinese are unwilling to assimilate into American society and to learn English. Over the years, this cultural self-segregation argument has grown into a fanciful theory; its rationale is that immigrant communities prosper economically through hard work and because of ethnic solidarity and that residents benefit from mutual-aid networks inside their ethnic enclaves. Thus, enclaves offer immigrants a new path to the middle class without the usual struggle through low-wage, dead-end jobs.

I have argued in this book that Chinese are attracted to Chinatown because of employment opportunities. Similar Asian and Hispanic enclaves exist across the country for the same reason. However, job availability should not be confused with easy upward mobility, nor should it be seen as the result of ethnic solidarity. Employment in ethnic enclaves is the product of America's post-industrial economy, in which American businesses have shifted their production to immigrant communities that provide cheap and unorganized labor. Investors have found their business ventures profitable and trouble-free in such enclaves. They leave their operations in the hands of strict Chinese managers who disregard American laws and labor regulations. Jobs within such ethnic enclaves are by definition low-wage and exploitative; they are a far cry from benevolent mutual-aid systems. What is worse, once immigrants are lured to Chinatown for jobs, they limit their chances to interact with American society and to learn English, which is essential for their economic mobility.

The ethnic-enclave thesis encourages continued segregation. It lends credibility to those who claim that today's American workers no longer have a strong work ethic or the spirit of self-reliance. It pits immigrants against American-born working people, intensifying the current anti-immigration sentiment and heightening racial tension. The ethnic-solidarity argument can also be used by American labor authorities as a rationale for not interfering in Chinatown affairs, for Chinese are said to be able to take care of themselves and not in need of government intervention. Yet this kind of indifference forces Chinatown residents to live in fear and to suffer degradation without recourse. In the 1990s, without the protection of labor-law enforcement, conditions in Chinatown are worse than ever. Violations such as home work, child labor, withholding back wages, and even indentured servitude are quite commonplace. The old claim that Chinese are unwilling to come forward to assist labor and law-enforcement authorities is simply not true. In recent years, the federal law-enforcement authorities which deal with organized crime have found that Chinese are more than willing to cooperate. When the FBI and DEA discovered the extent of Chinese involvement in the international heroin traffic in the mid-1980s, they made a concerted effort to reach out to the community for information and support. Many Chinese offered help once they realized that the authorities were committed to prosecution and willing to provide full protection to those who cooperated. Through successful indictment of drug traffickers, law-enforcement agencies were also able to master the Chinatown organized-crime networks. By 1995, the FBI and the New York district attorney offices had won convictions against a number of top tong leaders on charges of murder, extortion, drug trafficking, and money laundering, based on the RICO statute. The good news for the community is that the three most powerful tongs—An Leung, Hip Sing, and Tong An—have suffered dramatic defeats; the bad news is that more sophisticated international networks have since emerged to take their place in contract labor and human smuggling. Elimination of these new forces requires creative initiatives on the part of the police and the FBI and, certainly, the continued cooperation of the Chinese community.

While law enforcement against organized crime in Chinatown has gained strength, enforcement of labor law is nonexistent. Intervention by labor-law agencies in Chinatown is critical lest we allow conditions to deteriorate to nineteenth-century standards. Fortunately, the labor movement in Chinatown, meager as it may be and surviving against great odds, has never faltered. Today, many restaurant and garment workers have come to appreciate that their very livelihood is at stake. Workers at Silver Palace and Jing Fong restaurants succeeded in labor battles against their employers, and seamstresses at Wai Chang and other garment factories, most of whom were illegal, have succeeded in prosecuting employers who withhold back wages.

New immigrants now know that American unions have neither

the strength nor the incentive to represent them. Nor can they count on well-intentioned social welfare or legal defense groups to solve their problems. Real changes must therefore begin with grassroots organizing; only then will Americans pay attention to the plight of Chinese immigrants and only then will the U.S. Labor Department be forced to take action.

Underneath the appearance of ethnic cohesion, deep divisions have developed in Chinatown today. The community's struggles have begun to spill over into the larger society, as opposing sides recruit support from outside: social-service agencies are seeking the backing of the political parties, workers are soliciting help from rank-and-file union groups, tenant organizations are joining with outside neighborhood associations, and real-estate developers are lobbying City Hall for favorable zoning ordinances. Through these cross-ethnic alliances Chinatown is becoming tied in with the interests of American society at large and, as a result, my hope is that Chinatown in New York and elsewhere will ultimately become a more open and democratic neighborhood.

Notes

Introduction

1. U.S. Bureau of the Census (1993a, Table 3).
2. Charles Hirschman and Morrison G. Wong, "Trends in Socioeconomic Achievement among Immigrant and Native-Born Asian-Americans, 1960–1976," p. 511.
3. *Asian Americans for Equal Employment* (June 1977), p. 8.

Chapter 1

1. Stanford M. Lyman, *Chinatown and Little Tokyo*, p. 88.
2. Alexander Saxton, *The Indispensable Enemy*, p. 11.
3. Carey McWilliams, *California, the Great Exception*, p. 154.
4. Rose Hum Lee, *The Chinese in the United States of America*, p. 42.
5. "The Intelligentsia in Changing China," *Foreign Affairs* (January 1958), pp. 315–29.
6. Frederick Wakeman, Jr., *Strangers at the Gate*, p. 42.
7. Lyman, p. 47.

8. Ezra Vogel, *Canton under Communism*, p. 21.
9. Wakeman, p. 57.
10. Lee, p. 42.
11. *Chung-pao* [*Central Daily News*], May 14, 1985, p. 20.

Chapter 2

1. Paul Ong, "Chinatown Unemployment and the Ethnic Labor Market," p. 45.
2. Shepard Schwartz, "The Chinese Community of New York," pp. 50–51, 76.
3. C. T. Wu, "Chinese People and Chinatown in New York City," pp. 82–83.
4. *Měi-choū jih-pao*, May 8, 1963, p. 2.
5. Wu, p. 105.
6. *Měi-choū jih-pao*, September 30, 1962, p. 7; also in Stuart H. Cattell, *Health, Welfare and Social Organization in Chinatown*.
7. *The Chinatown Garment Industry Study*, p. 9.
8. *Ibid.*, p. 26.
9. *Ibid.*, p. 54.
10. *Ibid.*, p. 5.
11. See a similar discussion in Saskia Sassen-Koob, "Recomposition and Peripheralization at the Core," in *The New Nomads*, pp. 88–98.
12. *1984 New York Chinese Business Directory*.
13. *The Chinatown Garment Industry Study*, p. 98.

Chapter 3

1. Daniel Burstein, "Paper Dreams," *New York* (October 14, 1985).
2. *Chung-pao* [*Central Daily News*], June 28, 1985, p. 1.
3. *Ibid.*, September 18, 1985. Translated article from the *Los Angeles Times*, September 15, 1985; and *Shih-pao chōu-ká* [*News Weekly*], No. 9, 1985, pp. 10–11.
4. *Chung-pao*, September 10, 1986, p. 20.
5. See discussion in Michael A. Goldberg, *The Chinese Connection*, pp. 14–30.
6. Albert Scardino, "Commercial Rents in Chinatown Soar as Hong Kong Exodus Grows," *The New York Times*, December 24, 1986, pp. 45, 48.

7. *Chung-pao*, December 28, 1985, p. 20.

8. Department of Investigation, City of New York, "East-West Tower: Report of the Department of Investigation's Inquiry into Certain Events Preceding the Board of Estimate's Grant, on August 20, 1981, of a Special Zoning Permit . . ." 2137/81D (April 1982).

9. John Wang, "Developers Readying Three Towers in Chinatown," *The New York Times*, Section 8, September 20, 1981, p. 12.

10. *Chung-pao*, July 21, 1986, p. 20.

Chapter 4

1. *The Chinatown Garment Industry Study*, p. 115.

2. Ong, p. 45.

3. *Success of Asian Americans: Fact or Fiction?*, United States Commission on Civil Rights, Pub. 64 (September 1980), p. 13.

4. Yuan-li Wu, *The Economic Condition of Chinese Americans*, p. 54; Winifred Yu, "Asian-Americans Charge Prejudice Slows Climb to Management Ranks," *The Wall Street Journal*, Section 2, September 11, 1985, p. 35.

5. *Pěi-měi jih-pao* [*North America Daily News*], November 13, 1985, p. 8.

6. N. R. Kleinfield, "Mining Chinatown's Mountain of Gold," p. 8.

7. *The Chinatown Garment Industry Study*, p. 4.

8. Stanford Lyman, *Chinese Americans*, p. 133.

9. *Chung-pao*, January 22, 1987, p. 1.

10. *Ibid.*, March 21, 1985, p. 20.

11. *Ibid.*, February 8, 1985, p. 20.

12. *Ibid.*, March 26, 1985, p. 20.

13. *Ibid.*, November 30, 1985, p. 20.

14. Marlene Dixon, Susanne Jonas, and Ed McCaughan, "Reindustrialization and the Transnational Labor Force in the United States Today," pp. 101–14.

Chapter 5

1. John Watt, *The District Magistrate*, pp. 211–19.

2. Fei-Ling Davis, *Primitive Revolutionaries of China*, p. 54.

3. Maurice Freedman, *Lineage Organization in Southeastern China*, p. 114.

4. Watt, p. 211.

5. Him Mark Lai, "Historical Development of the Chinese Consolidated Benevolent Association/Huiguan System," in *Chinese America: History and Perspectives 1987*, pp. 13–51.
6. Schwartz, pp. 36–37.
7. *1949, By-laws of the Consolidated Chinese Benevolent Association*, New York.
8. *Hua-ch'iao jih-pao [China Daily News]*, December 14, 1984, p. 19; and in Ong Hsiang, "Chung-hua-kŭng-sŏ lu-pù-k'ai-chin pi-pēi-t'ao-t'ai" ["CCBA Reform or Perish"], in *Jen Yu Shih [People and Issues]*, Vol. 1, No. 13 (April 1, 1984), pp. 4–9.
9. *Mĕi-chōu jih-pao*, October 23, 1962, p. 8.
10. Peter Kwong, *Chinatown, New York*, p. 58.
11. Leong Gor Yun, *Chinatown Inside Out*, p. 58.
12. *Mĕi-chōu jih-pao*, January 10, 1962, p. 8.
13. *Pĕi-mĕi jih-pao [North American Daily News]*, March 12, 1986, p. 8; also *Jen Yu Shih [People and Issues]* (May 1, 1984), pp. 6–7.
14. Kwong, p. 112.
15. *Ibid.*, p. 128.
16. Lee, p. 169; and *Newsday*, June 30, 1959.
17. Trial brief on behalf of United States, "United States Court of Appeals for the Second Circuit, No. C 138–159, United States of America against *China Daily News*, Inc. and Eugene Moy," May 12, 1955.

Chapter 6

1. *Kúo-chi jih-pao [International Daily News]*, Los Angeles, February 10, 1987, p. 1.
2. Lee, p. 164.
3. Marvine Howe, "Chinatown Plan Is Key to Dispute," *The New York Times*, July 20, 1986, p. 22.
4. "Government's Version of the Offense—Introduction," document issued by The U.S. Attorney's Office for the Southern District of New York against members of Ghost Shadows, August 1986, p. 9.
5. *Ibid.*, p. 1.
6. *Ibid.*, pp. 8 and 13; *The New York Times*, July 20, 1986, p. 22.
7. *Chung-kúo shih-pao [China Times]*, October 25, 1984, p. 8.
8. *Chung-pao*, March 29, 1985, p. 20.
9. *Jen Yu Shih [People and Issues]*, Vol. 1, No. 15, June 1, 1984, p. 1.

10. Editorial by Lee Chan, "The Meaning of Official Bowing," *New York jih-pao* [*China Post*], September 15, 1985, p. 8.
11. Michael Daly, "The War for Chinatown," *New York* (February 14, 1983), p. 33.
12. *Ibid.*, p. 36.
13. *Jen Yu Shih*, April 25, 1983, Vol. 1, No. 3, back cover.
14. David Kaplan, David Goldberg, and Linda Jue, "Enter the Dragon," *San Francisco Focus* (1986), p. 76.
15. *Ibid.*
16. *The New York Times*, July 20, 1986, p. 22.
17. Sam Roberts, "A Chinatown Merchant Portrayed as Crime Boss," *The New York Times*, October 23, 1984, B3.
18. William Bastone, "Biaggi's $17,000 Loophole," *The Village Voice*, November 4, 1986, p. 15.
19. *President's Commission on Organized Crime: Organized Crime of Asian Origin*, record of Hearings III, October 23–25, 1984, New York, New York, pp. 93–94.
20. *Ibid.*, p. 103.
21. *Ibid.*, pp. 75–78.
22. *Szŭ-chièh jih-pao* [*The World Journal*], October 25, 1984, p. 1.
23. See public statement issued by the New York Chinese Press Association complaining about intimidations and threats received by their reporters. *Chung-pao*, April 23, 1985; and *Pĕi-mĕi jih-pao*, April 23, 1985, p. 16.
24. *Chung-kúo shih-pao*, October 25, 1984, p. 8.
25. *Chung-pao*, May 10, 1984, p. 12.
26. *Chung-kúo shih-pao*, November 2, 1984, p. 11.
27. *Chung-pao*, September 18, 1985; *Los Angeles Times*, September 15, 1985.

Chapter 7

1. *Chung-pao*, February 6, 1986, p. 20.
2. *Ibid.*, May 23, 1985, p. 20.
3. *Ibid.*
4. Kuo Chien-chi, *Hua-fŭ cheng-sang*, p. 120; and Shu Tu, *T'ang-jen-chièh ch'i-tan*, p. 26.
5. *Chung-pao*, February 25, 1985, p. 20.
6. *Ibid.*, February 26, 1985, p. 20.

7. *Ibid.*, August 7, 1986, p. 20.
8. Robert O. Boorstein, "One Chinese Youth's Path to a Jail in New York City," *The New York Times*, July 28, 1986, B1, 3.
9. *Chung-pao*, May 31, 1985, p. 20.
10. *Ibid.*, September 26, 1986, p. 20 and November 12, 1986, p. 20; and *Chung-kúo shih-pao*, November 2, 1984, p. 14.
11. See readers' letters to the editor in several local papers, such as the one from *Chung-pao*, September 10, 1985.

Chapter 8

1. Kwong, p. 89.
2. *Pĕi-mĕi jih-pao*, March 31, 1984, p. 8.
3. *Mĕi-chōu jih-pao*, June 14, 1966, p. 7.
4. "Teamsters Plan an Organizing Drive in Chinatown," *The New York Times*, May 13, 1979, p. 36; and *Szù-chiēh jih-pao*, May 13, 1979, p. 2.
5. *Kŭng-jen kuăn-tién* [*Workers Viewpoint*], May 4, 1980, p. 1.
6. *Hua-yü k'uài-pao* [*Sino Daily News*], July 5, 1980, p. 4.
7. Shiree Teng, "Women, Community and Equality," *East Wind* (Spring/Summer 1983), p. 20.
8. See discussion by Robert Laurentz, "Racial/Ethnic Conflict in the New York City Garment Industry, 1933–1980," p. 119.
9. See discussion by Herbert Hill of the similar kind of problems in the 1960s, "The ILGWU Today—The Decay of a Labor Union," pp. 3–14.
10. *Chung-pao*, November 29, 1985, p. 20.
11. *Ibid.*, December 1, 1985, p. 20.
12. *Ibid.*, June 21, 1986, p. 20; August 5, 1986, p. 20; and Scott Davis, "From Rags to Real Estate," *The Christian Science Monitor*, September 30, 1986, p. 6.
13. Leon Stein, ed., *Out of the Sweatshop*, Chapter 11, pp. 244–72.

Chapter 9

1. Lori Leong, "Personal Reflections on the Asian National Movements," *East Wind* (Spring/Summer 1982), pp. 31–34.
2. *Kŭng-jen kuăn-tién*, Vol. 2 No. 1, 1976, p. 35.

3. "1984 Elections and Political Power for Asian Americans," *East Wind* (Spring/Summer 1984), pp. 16–17.
4. *Asian Americans for Equality*, special issue, 1986, p. 1.
5. *Ibid.*
6. *Pĕi-mĕi jih-pao*, September 27, 1985, p. 12.
7. *Chung-pao*, February 8, 1986, p. 20.
8. Burstein, pp. 48–54.

Chapter 10

1. A legal work permit issued by the INS to those awaiting adjustment of immigration status or to those who have been apprehended for illegally entering the country and released on bail and are awaiting hearings.
2. The *Golden Venture* was a smuggling ship carrying some two hundred illegals from China that crashed off the Brooklyn shore in the spring of 1993.
3. A law passed in the state of California to cut off benefits to undocumented immigrants.
4. Min Zhou, *Chinatown: The Socioeconomic Potential of an Urban Enclave* p. 222.
5. *The New York Times*, March 12, 1995, p. 1; April 23, 1995.
6. See Vivian Huang and Tom Robbins, "Chinatown Wage War," *The Daily News*, April 20, 1995.

BIBLIOGRAPHY

BIBLIOGRAPHY OF PRIMARY SOURCES

1. Chinese-language newspapers

Chung-kúo shih-pao [*China Times*], New York City, 1982–84.
Chung-pao [*Central Daily News*], New York City, 1982–87.
Hua-ch'iao jih-pao [*China Daily News*], New York City, 1940–87.
Hua-yü k'uài-pao [*Sino Daily News*], New York City, 1980–86.
Kúo-chi jih-pao [*International Daily News*], Los Angeles, 1987.
Lién-ho jih-pao [*United Daily*], New York City, 1975–86.
Měi-chōu jih-pao [*Chinese Journal*], New York City, 1962–72.
New-York jih-pao [*China Post*], New York City, 1982–85.
Pěi-měi jih-pao [*North American Daily News*], New York City, 1978–86.
Sing-tao jih-pao [*Singtao Daily News*], New York City, 1980–84.
Szù-chièh jih-pao [*The World Journal*], New York City, 1983–87.

2. Chinese-language books

Cheng Sheng. *Hong-kong hēi-shè-hui huó-tùng chēn-hsiàng* [*Hong Kong Underworld*] (Hong Kong: Tien-ti Publications, 1984).

Chu Sin-liu. *Měi-kúo hua-fǔ* [*American Chinatown*] (New York: Chinese American Research Institute, 1985).

Chu Y. K. *Měi-kúo hua-ch'iao kai-shih* [*History of the Chinese People in America*] (New York: China Times Press, 1975).

Kuo Chien-chi. *Hua-fǔ cheng-sang* [*Life of Hardship in Chinatown*] (Hong Kong: Pu-i Publications, 1985).

Lee Yung. *Hua-fǔ pao-feng-yu* [*Storms in Chinatown*] (Hong Kong: Pu-i Publications, 1984).

Shu Tu. *T'ang-jen-chiēh ch'i-tan* [*Strange Stories of Chinatown*] (Taipei: Szu-chieh Publications, 1983).

Woo Shi-kang. *Láo-kūng wèn-tí mien-mien-kuan* [*All Aspects of Labor Issue*] (Hong Kong: Hua-feng Books, 1984).

Wu Hsu-lung. *Chung-i Ch'áng-chiu* [*Three-Hundred-Year History of the Green Gang*] (Taipei: Lung-chi Publications, 1986).

3. Chinese-language periodicals and pamphlets

Chinese American Restaurant Association of Greater New York, Inc. 1973–1985.

Hua-ch'iao Chih-kūng t'ung-hsin [*Chinese Staff and Workers Association News Letter*] 1980 on.

Hua Jen [*Overseas Chinese Monthly*], Hong Kong, 1985–86.

Jen Yu Shih [*People and Issues*] (New York: Chinatown Report Inc., 1983–87).

New York Chinese Business Directory (New York: Key Advertising Enterprises Inc., 1984).

Shih-pao chōu-ká [*News Weekly*] (New York: China Times, Inc., 1985)

Szù-chièh chōu-k'an [*World Journal East*] (New York: T. W. Wang Inc.).

4. English-language periodicals and pamphlets

Amerasia Journal, UCLA, Asian American Studies Center, 1971–87.

Bridge: The Asian American Magazine, New York City, 1971–85.

Bulletin of Concerned Asian Scholars, Vol. 4, No. 3 (Fall 1972).

East-West Journal, San Francisco, 1982–86.

East Wind: Politics and Culture of Asians in the U.S., San Francisco, 1982–86.

Forward: Journal of Socialist Thought, Oakland, California, Vol. 7, No. 1, 1987.

Getting Together, Oakland, California, 1971–77.

I Wor Kuen Journal, 1976.

Workers Viewpoint [*Kūng-jen kuǎn-tién*], 1976–80.

BIBLIOGRAPHY OF SECONDARY SOURCES

Asbury, Herbert. *The Gangs of New York* (New York: Alfred A. Knopf, 1927).

Banton, Michael. *The Social Anthropology of Complex Societies*, A.S.A. Monographs (New York: Tavistock Publications, 1966).

Blok, Anton. *The Mafia of a Sicilian Village, 1860–1960* (New York: Harper and Row, 1974).

Blythe, Wilfred. *The Impact of Chinese Secret Societies in Malaya* (London: Oxford University Press, 1969).

Bresler, Fenton. *The Trail of the Triads: An Investigation into International Crime* (London: Weidenfeld and Nicolson, 1980).

Bryce-Laporte, Roy Simon, ed. *Source Book on the New Immigration: Implications for the United States and the International Community* (New Brunswick, N.J.: Transaction Books, 1980).

Burstein, Daniel. "Paper Dreams," *New York*, October 14, 1985.

Caplovitz, David. *The Merchants of Harlem* (Beverly Hills, Calif.: Sage Publications, 1973).

Cattell, Stuart. *Health, Welfare and Social Organization in Chinatown* (New York: Community Service Society, 1970).

The Chinatown Garment Industry Study, by Abeles, Schwartz, Haeckel, and Silverblatt, Inc., study commissioned by Local 23–25 International Ladies Garment Workers Union and the New York Skirt and Sportswear Association, 1983.

Chinatown Study Group. *1969 Chinatown Study Group Report* (New York).

Chinese Historical Society of America. *Chinese America: History and Perspectives 1987* (San Francisco: Chinese Historical Society of America, 1987).

Chiswick, Barry, ed. *Gateways: U.S. Immigration Issues and Policies* (Washington: American Enterprise Institute for Public Policy Research, 1982).

City of New York. Department of investigation. *East-West Towers* (April 1982), 2137/81D.

Cohen, Allen B. "How to Meet Chinatown's Social Service and Education Needs," *The Chinese in America*. Sih, Paul K. T. and Leonard B. Allen, eds. No. 16 of Asia in the Modern World Series (New York: St. John's University Press, 1976).

Consolidated Chinese Benevolent Association. *1948 By-laws of the Consolidated Chinese Benevolent Association* (New York: CCBA).

Conversation of accused Bamboo Alliance members. Transcript of recording. Federal District Court, N.Y., April 17, 1985, Tape 5A.

Daley, Robert. *Year of the Dragon* (New York: Simon and Schuster, 1981).

Daly, Michael. "The War of Chinatown," *New York* (February 14, 1983).

Davis, Fei-Ling. *Primitive Revolutionaries of China* (Honolulu: The University Press of Hawaii, 1971).

Davis, Scott. "From Rags to Real Estate," *The Christian Science Monitor*, September 30, 1986.

Dillon, Richard H. *The Hatchet Men* (New York: Coward-McCann, 1962).

Dixon, Marlene, and Susanne Jonas, eds. *The New Nomads: From Immigrant Labor to Transnational Working Class*. Contemporary Marxism No. 5 (San Francisco: Synthesis Press, 1982).

Fessler, Loren W. ed., *Chinese in America* (New York: Vantage Press, Inc., 1983).

Fong, Mark Lau. *The Sociology of Secret Societies* (New York: Oxford University Press, 1981).

Freedman, Marcia. "The Labor Market for Immigrants in New York City," *New York Affairs*, 7:4 (1983).

Freedman, Maurice. *Lineage Organization in Southeastern China* (London: Athlone, 1958).

Gardner, Robert, Bryant Robey, and Peter C. Smith. "Asian Americans: Growth, Change, and Diversity." *Population Bulletin*, a publication of the Population Reference Bureau, Inc., Vol. 40, No. 4 (October 1985).

Glazer, Nathan. *Ethnic Dilemmas, 1964–1982* (Cambridge, Mass.: Harvard University Press, 1983).

Glick, Carl, and Hong Sheng-hwa. *Swords of Silence: Chinese Secret Societies—Past and Present* (New York: Whittlesey House, 1947).

Gold, Michael. *Jews Without Money* (New York: Avon Books, 1961).

Goldberg, Michael A. *The Chinese Connection* (Vancouver: University of British Columbia Press, 1985).

Gong, Eng Ying, and Bruce Grant. *Tong War!* (New York: Nicholas L. Brown, 1930).

Gordon, David M. *Segmented Work, Divided Workers* (New York: Cambridge University Press, 1982).

"Government's Version of the Offense—Introduction" (charges against members of Ghost Shadows). The U.S. Attorney's Office for the Southern District of New York, August 1986.

Hart, Robert Lamb, Adam Kriratsy, and William Stuben. *Chinatown, New York* (New York City Department of City Planning, July 1968) (pamphlet).

Hawkins, Brett W., and Robert A. Lorinskas. *The Ethnic Factor in American Politics* (Columbus, Ohio: Charles E. Merrill Publishing Co. 1970).

Heyer, Virginia. "Patterns of Social Organization in New York City's Chinatown." Unpublished doctoral dissertation, Columbia University, 1953.

Higham, John, ed. *Ethnic Leadership in America* (Baltimore: Johns Hopkins University Press, 1978).

Hill, Herbert. "The ILGWU Today—The Decay of a Labor Union," *New Politics* (Summer 1962).

Hirschman, Charles, and Morrison G. Wong. "Socio-economic Gains of Asian Americans, Blacks and Hispanics, 1960–1976," *American Journal of Sociology*, Vol 90, #3 (November 1984).

———. "Trends in Socioeconomic Achievement among Immigrant and Native-Born Asian-Americans, 1960–1976," *The Sociological Quarterly*, 22 (Autumn 1981).

Kaplan, David E., Donald Goldberg, and Linda Jue. "Enter the Dragon." *San Francisco Focus*, 1986.

Kleinfield, N. R. "Mining Chinatown's Mountain of Gold," *The New York Times*, June 1, 1986, Section 3, pp. 1, 8.

Kritz, Mary M., Charles B. Keely, and Silvano M. Tomasi. *Global Trends in Migration: Theory and Research on International Population Movements* (Staten Island, New York: Center for Migration Studies, 1981).

Kuo Chia-ling. *Social and Political Change in New York's Chinatown* (New York: Praeger, 1977).

Kwong, Peter. *Chinatown, New York: Labor and Politics, 1930–1950* (New York: Monthly Review Press, 1979).

———. "Boycott Dewey Wong," *The Guardian*. July 25, 1984.

———. "Who Rules Chinatown?" *The Guardian*. March 27, 1985.

Laurentz, Robert. "Racial/Ethnic Conflict in the New York City Garment Industry, 1933–1980." Ph.D. dissertation, SUNY/Binghamton, 1980.

Lee, Rose Hum. *The Chinese in the United States of America* (Hong Kong: Hong Kong University Press, 1960).

Leichter, Franz S. *The Return of the Sweatshop: A Call for State Action.* October 1979 (pamphlet).

———. *Sweatshops to Shakedowns: Organized Crime in New York's Garment Industry.* March 1982.

Leong, Gor Yun. *Chinatown Inside Out* (New York: Barrows Mussey, 1936).

Light, Ivan H. *Ethnic Enterprise in America: Business and Welfare among Chinese, Japanese, and Blacks* (Berkeley: University of California Press, 1972).

Lum, Joann. "Chinatown: A Community Grapples with Its Future," *City Limits* (New York: November 1985).

Lyman, Stanford M. *Chinese Americans* (New York: Random House, 1974).

———. *The Asian in the West.* Social Science & Humanities Publication No. 4 (Reno: Western Studies Center, University of Nevada System, 1970).

———. *Chinatown and Little Tokyo: Power, Conflict, and Community among Chinese and Japanese Immigrants in America* (New York: Associated Faculty Press, Inc., 1986).

McWilliams, Carey. *California, the Great Exception* (New York: Current Books, Inc., 1949).

Mattera, Philip. *Off the Books: The Rise of the Underground Economy* (New York: St. Martin's Press, 1985).

New York Chinese Business Directory. 1984 edition (New York: Key Advertising Enterprises, Inc.).

New York State Advisory Committee to the U.S. Commission on Civil Rights, *The Forgotten Minority: Asian Americans in New York City*, 1977.

Ong, Paul. "Chinatown Unemployment and the Ethnic Labor Market," *Amerasia Journal.* Asian American Studies, UCLA, 11:1 (1984), pp. 35–54.

Portes, Alejandro, and Robert L. Bach. *Latin Journey: Cuban and Mexican Immigrants in the United States* (Berkeley: University of California Press, 1985).

———. "Immigrant Earning: Cuban and Mexican Immigrants in the United States," *International Migration Review* 14 (Fall 1980), pp. 315–41.

President's Commission on Organized Crime: Organized Crime of Asian Origin, record of Hearing III, October 23–25, 1984, New York, N.Y. Washington, D.C., Superintendent of Documents, U.S. Government Printing Office.

Sassen-Koob, Saskia. "The International Circulation of Resources and De-velopment: The Case of Migrant Labor," *Development and Change*, 9:4 (October 1978).

Saxton, Alexander. *The Indispensable Enemy: Labor and the Anti-Chinese Movement in California* (Berkeley: University of California Press, 1971).

Schwartz, Shepard. "The Chinese Community of New York," unpublished manuscript, Columbia University, Research in Contemporary Cul-tures.

Scott, David Clark. "Chinatown Rags to Real Estate," *The Christian Science Monitor*. September 30, 1986.

Sowell, Thomas. *Ethnic America: A History* (New York: Basic Books, 1981).

Stein, Leon, ed. *Out of the Sweatshop* (New York: Quadrangle, 1977).

Steinberg, Stephen. *The Ethnic Myth: Race, Ethnicity, and Class in America* (Boston: Beacon Press, 1981).

Sung, Betty Lee. *Mountain of Gold: The Story of the Chinese in America* (New York: Macmillan, 1967).

———. *Chinese Population in Lower Manhattan, 1978*. U.S. Department of Labor Employment and Training Administration, Washington (pam-phlet).

Tanzi, Vito, ed. *The Underground Economy in the United States and Abroad* (Lexington, Mass.: Lexington Books, 1982).

Thompson, Richard H. "Ethnicity versus Class: Analysis of Conflict in a North American Chinese Community," *Ethnicity* (1979).

———. "The State and the Ethnic Community: The Changing Social Or-ganizations of Toronto's Chinatown." Ph.D. dissertation, University of Michigan, 1979.

United States Commission on Civil Rights. *Civil Rights Issues of Asian and Pacific Americans: Myths and Realities* (Washington, D.C.: U.S. Print-ing Office, 1980).

———. *Success of Asian Americans: Fact or Fiction?* (Washington, D.C.: Clear-inghouse Publication 64, September 1980).

Vogel, Ezra. *Canton under Communism* (New York: Harper and Row, 1969).

Wakeman, Frederick Jr. *Strangers at the Gate: Social Disorder in South China, 1839–1861* (Berkeley: University of California Press, 1966).

Walzer, Michael, Edward T. Kantowicz, John Higham, and Mona Harrington. *The Politics of Ethnicity* (Cambridge: Harvard University Press, 1982).

Wang, John. "Behind the Boom: Power and Economics in Chinatown," *New York Affairs* (Spring 1979).

———. *The New York Times*, Section B, September 20, 1981, pp. 1, 12.

Wang, Y. C. "The Intelligentsia in Changing China," *Foreign Affairs* (January 1958).

Watson, James. *Emigration and the Chinese Lineage* (Berkeley: University of California Press, 1975).

Watt, John Robertson. *The District Magistrate in Late Imperial China* (New York: Columbia University Press, 1972).

Wilson, Kenneth L., and Alejandro Portes. "Immigrant Enclaves: An Analysis of the Labor Market Experiences of Cubans in Miami," *American Journal of Sociology* (September 1980).

Wu Cheng Tsu. "Chinese People and Chinatown in New York City." Ph.D. dissertation, Clark University, 1958.

Wu Yuan-li, ed. *The Economic Condition of Chinese Americans* (Chicago: Pacific/Asian American Mental Health Research Center, Monograph, 1980).

Yu Winifred. "Asian-Americans Charge Prejudice Slows Climb to Management Ranks," *The Wall Street Journal*, September 11, 1985, Section 2, p. 35.

INDEX

NOTE: To avoid duplication, Chinatown, regardless of location, has been treated as one entity. Also, in other entries, the word Chinatown has been omitted (for example, gentrification, *not* gentrification in Chinatown).

tongs, crimes and activities of (*cont.*)
    fect of on Chinatown, 122–3, 127–
    9; government and, 122–5, 127,
    129; IWK and, 164; and gangs, *see*
    gangs
travel agencies, price war among, 68
Triads, 89, 97, 119
Tsai, Jerry, 60
Tse, Alice, 152

Uncle Seven, *see* Eng
Uncle Tai's, organization of, 141
unions, 14, 78, 123, 138, 147, 159,
    173; and Chinatown workers, 8, 13,
    30–1, 62, 64–5, 77–8, 102–4, 123,
    137–59, 171; *see also names of*, gar-
    ment industry, laundries, *and* restau-
    rants
United Orient Bank, 117, 127–8
United States, Chinese students and,
    15–16, 59–62; and cold war, 104;
    and Chinese Nationalists, 104–5; ser-
    vices of, to Chinatown, 105–7; and
    tongs, 122–5; and gangs, 125, 128–
    9; and People's Republic, *see* People's
    Republic
United States Census, of 1980, 25–6,
    58; of 1970, 57
United States Commission on Civil
    Rights, 1980 report of, 60

United States Immigration and Natu-
    ralization Services, 23, 40
Uptown, 5, 22, 35, 58–62, 73–4

Vietnam, Chinese immigrants from, 4,
    40, 112; opposition to war with,
    161

Wang An, 60
Wang, Y.C ., study by, 16
War Brides Act, 20, 29
Westinghouse Science Talent Search,
    73
Williams, David, 119
women, and garment industry, 26,
    29–32, 35, 150; 155–6; and New
    York City Chinatown, 29; and union
    affairs, 152–3, 157–8; *see also*
    ILGWU
Woo, S. B., 113–14, 168–9
Workers' Viewpoint, 164
World War II, and Chinese in U.S., 20

Yang Chen Ning, 69
Year of the Dragon, 116–17, 132
youth, future of, 70–1; and education,
    71–6; job opportunities for, 72;
    problems of, 74–6, 110, 120, 131;
    harassment of, 105–6; perks of,
    111–12, 120; and Project Reach,
    131; and gangs, *see* gangs